A Woman's Guide to Working for Herself

Inspiration, information and
advice from women who
run their own business for women
who aspire to do so

SANDRA HEWETT

howtobooks

Published by How To Books Ltd,
Spring Hill House, Spring Hill Road,
Begbroke, Oxford OX5 1RX
Tel: (01865) 375794. Fax: (01865) 379162
info@howtobooks.co.uk
www.howtobooks.co.uk

How To Books greatly reduce the carbon footprint of their books by sourcing their typesetting and
printing in the UK.

British Library Cataloguing in Publication Data
A catalogue record for this book is available from the British Library

ISBN: 978 1 84528 412 1

Produced for How To Books by Deer Park Productions, Tavistock, Devon
Typeset by PDQ Typesetting, Newcastle-under-Lyme, Staffs.
Printed and bound in Great Britain by Bell & Bain Ltd, Glasgow

NOTE: The material contained in this book is set out in good faith for general guidance and no
liability can be accepted for loss or expense incurred as a result of relying in particular circumstances
on statements made in the book. Laws and regulations are complex and liable to change, and readers
should check the current position with the relevant authorities before making personal arrangements.

Contents

Acknowledgements

The Womens in Business Clubs for the enthusiasm of their members (many listed below) in offering case studies:

Women working for themselves

Robin Bradley, co-founder, Phoenix Trading, www.phoenix-trading.co.uk

Charlotte Carr, Kiddy Cook franchisee

Lisa Cole, Lactivist www.lactivist.co.uk www.lactivistbling.co.uk

Nikki Geddes, Kiddy Cook Franchising www.kiddycook.co.uk

Alex Glover, Usborne Books www.usborne.com/sell-usborne-books/home-business-opportunity.aspx

Elizabeth Gooch, eg Solutions www.eguk.co.uk

Tabitha Harman, Mimimyne www.mimimyne.com

Wendy Howard, Spirit of Venus Limited www.spiritofvenus.co.uk

Yana Johnson, MBE, Yana Cosmetics www.yanacosmetics.com

Lorna Knapman, Love Food Festival www.lovefoodfestival.com

Emma Lodge, Balance Accounting Solutions www.balanceaccountingsolutions.co.uk

Sally MacMillan, Ask Sally

Karen Mattison, Women Like Us www.womenlikeus.org.uk

Sue May, Independent Phoenix Trader

Corinne McLavy, Zero3 Marketing www.zero3marketing.co.uk

Kavita Oberoi, Oberoi Consulting www.oberoi-consulting.com

Cari Parker, Coochie Cou www.coochiecou.co.uk

Cherry Parsons, CJ Motor Repairs www.cjmotorrepairs.co.uk

Emma Pearce, Pearce Marketing www.pearcemarketing.co.uk

Karen Purves, Centre for Effective Marketing www.havemoreclients.com

Claudine Reid MBE, PJs Community Services www.patreid.co.uk

Jackie Roberts, The Chocolate Tailor www.chocolatetailor.co.uk

Samantha Russell, Sardine Design www.sardinedesign.com

Karen Sherr, Musical Minis Limited www.musicalminis.co.uk

Karen Standen, Four Paws Aqua www.fourpawsaqua.co.uk

Jane Stretton, Dove Farm www.dovefarm.co.uk

Janice Taylor, Blue Sky Career Consulting www.blueskycareerconsulting.co.uk

Kaye Taylor, SK Chase www.skchase.com

Kristina Thomas, Sussex Local Magazine www.sussexlocal.net
Mary Thomas, Concise Training www.concisetraining.net

Support organisations

Richard Berry, director, Direct Selling Association
Simone Brummelhuis, founder of thenextwoman.com
Business Link www.businesslink.gov.uk and Barclays Bank www.barclays.co.uk/
    business for their kind permission to reproduce website copy
Professor Sara Carter, head of department, Hunter Centre for Entrepreneurship at
    the University of Strathclyde
Tom Endean, marketing manager, British Franchise Association
The Federation of Small Businesses
Gill Fennings-Monkman, director of Prowess and consultant director of Newham
    Women's Business Centre
Rebecca Harding, managing director, Delta Economics
Katherine Harvey, Social Enterprise Coalition
Juliet Hope, chief executive, Startup
Bev Hurley, founder and chief executive of Enterprising Women
Annabel Kirk, The Prince's Trust
Pete Lewis, Leonard Cheshire Disability
Mark Lywood, Prime
Ian Robertson, chief executive, National Council for Graduate Entrepreneurship
Chris Simpson, account manager, Business Link Northeast

Preface

So you are thinking of working for yourself? It's a great step to take but can be daunting if you are used to a regular pay cheque and value teamwork. This book aims to provide you with the information, inspiration and motivation that will help you make one of the most important decisions of your life.

It takes you from your starting point, recognising that there is no 'one size fits all' blueprint, just because you are a woman. For instance:

■ You may wish to work a 20-hour week from home or you may have ambitions to build a business with a multi-million pound turnover.

■ You could run a market stall, a franchise or a social enterprise: all very different types of business.

■ You may be unemployed, disabled, a new mum, young or old. There are organisations that can help get you into self employment.

Getting support

There is support for business start-ups in the form of Business Link, online and there is also now a myriad websites and networking organisations to help you start or grow your venture. Some of these are tailored to women. The amount of support varies around the country, but you will find many of these listed in the Appendix section.

Finding your motivation

Female entrepreneurs are shown to be as successful as their male counterparts, but they often bring different approaches to business. The profit motive is cited less often by women setting up businesses and many now have an eye to community benefit as well as work/life balance. You'll find lots of ideas and inspiration here.

Boosting your earnings

The majority of women who work for themselves work solo: self employed. Much of the focus of this book is on them. They are freelance or contractors, beauticians, home workers, direct selling agents, 'mumpreneurs' and webpreneurs. They don't employ staff and they don't have any debt outside of family/ friends and their credit cards. But don't think this is for pin money: these women can earn far greater than the average wage.

Managing risk

Plenty of women, though, are prepared to take on risk and build a business. Female entrepreneurs are now found in every sector of the economy. We will hear from some of them and explore what it takes to follow in their footsteps.

Joining the big girls and boys

Perhaps you have the drive and ambition to join the smaller group of women who have developed major companies and become millionaires. Growth on this scale isn't the main focus of this book but there is a section devoted to what it takes to be a 'tycoon'.

Learning from others

However, it is the women who have told their stories here who make this book. Every one has a lesson to offer and they have been incredibly honest in recounting their struggles, both personal and business, as well as their successes. You will avoid many pitfalls as a result of reading these!

How to use this book

You don't have to read this book from cover to cover. You can jump to the sections of interest to you. Have paper and pencil to make notes and reflect on what rings true for you; try some of the exercises. But do study the nuts and bolts: the serious stuff, the business planning, managing finance and marketing. These are fundamentals to any enterprise, large or small. Hopefully, you will find them accessible and be encouraged to sit down and apply them to your venture.

Most of all, this book aims to give you motivation and courage. Working for yourself isn't easy and in a recession it can be scary. But for the right person it's the only way to work.

Part 1:
Getting Started

Introduction

Women set up in business for many reasons. What you do and how well you thrive will depend on your circumstances, your motivation, your drive and the support you have. It's because of such diversity that this book will look at the variety of backgrounds women come from and the options you have in working for yourself. It is divided into three, broad categories:

- Being an expert in a field that offers the opportunity to go freelance or become a contractor. This can be seen as a pull reason (opportunistic). You may also have hit the 'glass ceiling' in the corporate environment.

- Having a burning passion or talent, or spotting a market opportunity and setting up a new business. This is also a pull reason (ambition, desire) although a big push can come in the form of a windfall payment or a partner to support you.

- Wanting or needing to get back into the workforce after a break, such as unemployment or maternity leave. This is more of a push reason. You may not yet know what you want to do, but self employment would fit your lifestyle better than employment – and may be the only option.

Whatever your circumstances, you'll need determination and help to join the one million plus women who work for themselves in the UK.

CHAPTER ONE

WHY DO YOU WANT TO WORK FOR YOURSELF?

Be sure this is for you

Before you get going, be clear about why you want to become self employed. One reason to pause is that the road is going to be bumpy at times; you will have moments of questioning, self doubt and anxiety. If you can't answer the question, 'Why did I start this?' it won't be so easy to get through. However, being able to remind yourself of the embryonic motivation can help keep you on track and remain inspired. It will also help in your decision making along the way.

TRY THIS

Here are some common motivations, with challenges that could happen. Think of your main motivations and the challenges you might face.

Reason for starting up	Challenge – so what if...
Earn more money	You're not making money in 12 months?
Be your own boss	You are at the beck and call of clients?
Flexibility of hours	You are working 24/7?
Can better exploit talent/expertise	The work is low grade (but pays well)?
Can't get a job	You can't work alone?
Suits lifestyle	It doesn't!
Know others who do it	They all seem to be doing better than you?
Want a challenge	It gets scary?
Want fun	You can't find this fun?
Have set-up capital	It's not enough?
Long-held ambition	It just seems like drudgery?
The best career move	You're out of the loop?
I have this great idea!	You can't find the market for it?

Be realistic

Even if your determination is rock solid (great!), challenging yourself with 'what ifs', perhaps with a friend or partner, will test your ideas. You needn't get doom laden: we can leave climate change, terrorist threat and the collapse of the economy to the insurers.

But be realistic, if not slightly pessimistic, on the possible pitfalls business-wise, financially and emotionally. The wonder of spreadsheets is that you can do different financial scenarios at the press of a button. (You need to develop your own 'software' for the emotional scenarios!)

> ❝ *I wanted a better quality of life really, a more relaxed way of working, ideally from home. My husband works shifts and we just never saw each other as, often, the times he would be off, I would be in Bristol or Birmingham, hardly on the doorstep to where we live.* ❞
>
> Sally MacMillan, Ask Sally

> ❝ *Despite the conflicts with family demands there are great benefits of being self-employed. I can rearrange my working time to suit my needs and do not need to answer to anyone. I don't need to face difficult conversations with bosses about my child being ill or not wanting to work at a certain time. I know I will still meet all my commitments by working in the evening instead.* ❞
>
> Emma Pearce, Pearce Marketing Consultants

> ❝ *I am not an employee! I like to do my own thing which is generally not tolerated in organisations. So it was only a matter of time before I needed to spread my wings.* ❞
>
> Karen Purves, Centre for Effective Marketing

We will look at personality traits in Chapter 5 and risk in Chapters 3 and 13.

Working round the family

According to Chris Simpson, an account manager with Business Link in the northeast of England, the most common reason why women want to work for themselves is family. Our working life does not make it easy for a parent (most likely the mum) to work around school and childcare hours. So, many women look at the hours they want to work, where they want to do it and then find their own work to fit those requirements.

❛ I probably would not have gone it alone, if my (employer) had been more flexible with my work hours. ❜

Janice Taylor, Blue Sky Career Consulting

Be adaptable

However, as Chris points out, being your own boss can still create stresses. The most popular sector for the women he sees is beauty, including hair dressing and complementary therapies. 'It sounds like a job you can do when you like, but clients want the appointment when they want it, not when it suits you,' he says.

❛ Work consumed me and my time; it created conflict with my children. But they remained supportive throughout it all. ❜

Karen Purves, Centre for Effective Marketing

❛ I thought it would be easy actually, which goes to show how inexperienced I was! Right now I am typing this from an internet cafe with my two boys because I am waiting for a new broadband connection at home. Luckily I have skills, such as writing copy, editing images and writing HTML, which means I can do a lot myself. I work fast and am good at concentrating. However, I find doing shows and exhibitions difficult and getting to events in the evening can be a nightmare, so I've scaled down the amount of things that I do. ❜

Tabitha Harman, Mimimyne

How important is money?

How much is money – earnings – a motivator for starting up a business? Most people want to earn at least a living wage, but if you were asked how you intend to maximise your profit, would you have an answer? Do you take finance seriously?

As some of our case studies show, your attitude to your business and money is linked to confidence and self image. Many of these women will inspire you to take a more serious approach to your business.

Again, Chris Simpson of Business Link has observed that, on the whole, women have lower expectations about profit than men. They usually start their business on a smaller scale and are prepared to sacrifice higher earnings for flexibility. According to Chris, 'The man is still the main breadwinner in many families, so many women's income, though important, is a supplement and not necessarily a living wage.'

❝ *The financial success of the business is certainly a significant aim and part of the business – we all need to pay our bills, but I would rather work for less and have a better quality of life than earn a fortune and be stressed out.* ❞
Corinne McLavy, Director Zero3 Marketing

❝ *I had a very supportive partner. I wasn't the main breadwinner – it was just a chance to "go for it".* ❞
Janice Taylor, Blue Sky Career Consulting

❝ *My ultimate ambition is to earn enough money to allow my husband to downsize. I have been self-sufficient to date and the money that I earn through my face-to-face work has supported my new online business.* ❞
Mary Thomas, Concise Training

Take advantage of life's changes

On the plus side, this does give women with partners, at least in more affluent households, the opportunity to take a risk that the man might not take. As Chris Simpson puts it, 'Women are more likely to have a life-changing event than men and go into something they have wanted to do for a long time. They have that little push.'

The main life-changing event, of course, is starting a family. The woman is more likely to leave her job – not always voluntarily – after a baby than the man. But women can also get start-up finance from redundancy or inheritance.

Hitting the glass ceiling

Some women start working for themselves for less positive reasons, when they find their career development is stifled. But, after the initial disappointment or resentment, you can find real freedom. Self employment can remove the barriers or discrimination of the corporate world and take off the brake on earnings.

❝ *My "get away" motivation was purely to get off the corporate ladder and simply being a cog in the wheel with someone else pushing the buttons. The lack of motivation and "energy" in the corporate world really started to dampen my naturally bright enthusiasm.* ❞
Wendy Howard, Spirit of Venus

Make it look good

With confidence and a professional appearance, many women will achieve more working for themselves than in employment. Chris Simpson explains why having 'Director' on the business card or 'Limited' in your business name all add weight. You could be working from a small bedroom at home, but if you have a professional manner, good literature and website, you can have more authority. It's about your appearance to the outside world.'

The sad thing for many people is that they are miserable in their jobs and have no power or opportunity to change this.

> ❛ *I was thoroughly miserable in my previous role as duty manager. Although I was capable of doing the job, I found the experience draining both physically and emotionally. Job satisfaction was sporadic, there was pressure to meet sales targets, I led a poorly paid, demotivated team and I worked extra unpaid hours on a daily basis.* ❜
>
> Kristina Thomas, Sussex Local Magazine

CHAPTER TWO

WHAT DO YOU WANT YOUR LIFESTYLE TO BE?

How will your venture fit in with the rest of your life *and* provide you with the standard of living you want?

' *My greatest challenge is living within my means! Without a regular salary I do not have so much disposable income. But I am much happier and fulfilled; there is something very satisfying in making your living by producing something that people enjoy. I live on a much lower income but I still have a good standard of living.* '

Jackie Roberts, The Chocolate Tailor

' *My "towards" motivation was "freedom" to spend my life doing something worthwhile with people who really appreciated what I had to offer them. Also, flexibility to start my day when I want to, take my girls to school, walk my dog and go to the gym. I catch up by working in the evenings if I want to. Financially, I knew I'd never be rich working for someone else and if I didn't change, I'd run out of life before I achieved any real financial success.* '

Wendy Howard, Spirit of Venus

Plan your hours

Many women going it alone need to work around a family, which means juggling daytime hours and school holidays. You may want to work locally and web-based, which keeps the travelling to a minimum. Conversely, you might have good support or a lack of ties and desire international travel. So how will you achieve this lifestyle?

In Chapter 1 we saw how the reality can be different from your vision. You daren't turn down work at the beginning of your venture. But what started as a four-day week with a study course on the fifth day and stress-free weekends could become six days a week, getting invoices out until 9pm. And when you do see family and friends, you are worn out.

How do we balance work/life?

Business advisers will rightly suggest you prepare your business plan, which sets out your vision, output targets and financial forecasts (see Chapter 16). It is also worth investing time thinking about what you want from this business *and* what you don't want. What are your boundaries?

TRY THIS
- ▶ Write down what fulfilment means for you.
- ▶ What are your priorities – income, family, time for yourself, achievement?
- ▶ Plan a week's calendar with your ideal hours of work, family and social time. How realistic do you think it is?

What are your needs and values?
For instance:
- ▶ 'I want more challenge from my work.'
- ▶ 'I don't want to be stuck at home only ever talking by email.'
- ▶ 'I want to drive less to keep my carbon footprint down.'
- ▶ 'I have medical needs and have to restrict my hours.'

Make a note of anything that is important for your business plan.

Make sure it is flexible

If your lifestyle demands are fixed (like the medical one above) you have to be sure your business has flexibility. This may be a case of setting boundaries and saying 'No' when too much work comes in, or to another overseas trip. Be realistic about your potential income within these boundaries and make sure you still have a viable business. If you have only 20 hours a week to work but you won't be in profit unless you work 25, you will need to rethink.

Develop quality work

Another trap is to fill your time on work that is easy to get and to do. If you don't allow yourself time to develop your reputation and your skills, you could find yourself unfulfilled and with a business that doesn't develop, or become cutting edge. These are the first businesses to go under when markets change or recession hits.

Can you keep to your boundaries?

It is highly likely that when you set up in business the boundaries of your work and your home life blur. This may be because you are working from home (see

Chapter 24) or you take work home. If you are working part time it's difficult to tell clients to phone between the hours of 9am and 3pm, so the mobile and Blackberry can encroach on family life. And, of course, your heart and soul will be in it so it's difficult to switch off the computer, shut the door and go off on that weekly country walk you put in your plan!

❝ *There are never enough hours in the day and always conflicting demands. I try not to work in the evenings but do work during the weekend. I would like to get to a stage where I can justify a cleaner which would take some of the pressure off. The dog seems to be getting fewer walks than usual at the moment too; this is good thinking time so I do like doing this.* ❞

Mary Thomas, Concise Training

❝ *52.2% of female-run businesses report an average working week of over 48 hours.* ❞

Work-Life Balance, survey of members, Federation of Small Businesses, 2008[1]

Get help

If work/life balance is decidedly unbalanced and causing you stress, talk to an adviser or hire a coach. Talking through your options with an objective and experienced outsider can turn things around. There are also many self-coaching books and books on time management which could help.

Be a Jill of all trades!

Have you been spoilt by corporate life? Your computer goes down so you just pick up the phone and IT fixes it within a couple of hours. You need a press release, so you just contact the PR department. HR, facilities management, print room, finance, canteen . . . hello? They're all YOU now! Do you have the time and expertise to do it all? Probably not.

The successful woman working for herself must gather a circle of reliable suppliers around her. You must be able to trust them, so it helps if you have known them for a while. But beware: friends don't always make the best suppliers. Networking is great for finding the help you need, as well as getting referrals.

‘ *On the day-to-day admin, I do nearly everything myself but have help from my computer support company (who can troubleshoot computer problems) and my accountant and freelance bookkeepers. I would like to have a business partner one day, but I haven't met the right person yet.* ’

Tabitha Harman, Mimimyne

There are tips about hiring and working with suppliers in Chapter 21, plus a dire lesson from one of our case studies in Chapter 10.

CHAPTER THREE

GETTING PAST FEAR AND PROCRASTINATION

So . . . your analysis and reflection has not dimmed your resolve. You have the opportunity and the talent and you believe that your business will fit within your lifestyle. But you are still delaying . . . what is holding you back?

> ❝ *I deliberately left it until after Christmas so I could get that out the way, as my partner was keen for me to leave earlier. I was on a three-month period of notice and used this time to get my head straight and start to set up a few things.* ❞
>
> Janice Taylor, Blue Sky Career Consulting

Ah yes, procrastination. (Maybe I'll finish this chapter later . . .)

Get your act together

The dictionary definition of procrastination is 'to defer action'. Most of us put off doing unpleasant or boring jobs. How many mums (or dads) berate their child for not doing their homework while ignoring the pile of ironing building up in the basket?

But starting your new business is neither unpleasant nor boring, is it? And while some procrastinators are lazy or lack self discipline, this is unlikely to apply to someone really motivated to set up their business.

> ❝ *I procrastinated over Coochie Cou. It was an idea that I discussed and mulled over for ages before actually going ahead and booking my first venue. A good friend helped me get going by contacting the venue for me to find out details; well after that I just had to go and book, didn't I?* ❞
>
> Cari Parker, The Dales Party Company

There is another reason: *fear of failure*. We put so much of ourselves into this venture that if we struggle or, indeed, fail, it seems like a blow to us personally and professionally. So perhaps we keep doing research, redo our business plan and continue in the comfort of our secure if humdrum job. This is entirely understandable, and it's not as simple as saying, '*Just do it!*'

> ❛ *I had fear like never before!! No one can tell you what it is like to step over that line and suddenly lose all the security you've taken for granted and been "programmed" to expect.* ❜
>
> Wendy Howard, Spirit of Venus

Dealing with fear

There is a coaching question to tackle this: 'What's the worst thing that can happen?' It's a risky one, though, because the client can then go into a spiral of catastrophising, and before you know it she is convinced the business will lose her the house, husband, kids and cat! A fear is never to be dismissed, especially when it is holding you up. But getting things in perspective, doing some financial planning (see Chapter 16) and considering risk will help. (Surely, the cat would never leave you!)

Wendy Howard, Director of leadership training company Spirit of Venus, recognises this: 'Procrastination can occur even when you don't recognise it as such. Often you find yourself doing something mundane such as checking your emails again and again. Or tidying the office rather than doing those follow-up calls.

I am convinced this causes many failures in business, as people procrastinate in so many ways but don't recognise it's fear that's the problem, I really go into this on my training programme and people are often amazed to discover their "block" and why.'

Some tips for dealing with procrastination
- Good research and advice (see Chapter 4) can do a lot to boost your confidence.
- Get support from friends, coach or an adviser; let them know you are in avoidance mode and need to be challenged, coaxed or encouraged.
- Break down initial tasks into small chunks.
- Set goals and deadlines so they don't seem overwhelming and endless.
- Recognise and celebrate achievements.

So hey, get back here, the dog can wait for its walk!

Do some scenario planning

Scenario planning isn't just for financial spreadsheets. You can turn other aspects of your planning into scenarios so you can begin to get a feel of how operating would be like. (If you are a number cruncher, you could go into decision tree analysis, but that's the subject of a specialist book.)

Let's take a fictitious Carol, who works in a human resources (HR) department and who is thinking of going freelance, offering interim (temporary) HR support. Ideal for businesses that have short-term resource needs, maternity cover etc. What objections would a nervous Carol put up and how could she answer those objections?

I might not get work
A: I'm going to do my research talk to my employer (maybe) and other contacts and ask if they use interims; and if so, what kind of person/experience/ qualification are they looking for? Would I fit that bill? I can talk to specialist recruitment agencies about the market, rates and types of jobs currently available. I can find out what work I could do and where I could be working.

I'm not experienced/qualified enough
A: Again, I can talk to potential clients and agencies. If I'm right, I can think about getting more qualifications, or perhaps move job to gain the right experience. I'm going to think long term.

I couldn't risk being unemployed
A: Well, I know some freelancers in the HR field whom I can talk to about work flow. And there is a professional body I can get a view from. Many freelancers earn enough to tide themselves over a month or two without work – in fact, that bloke I talked to last month went away for three months every summer, lucky ***! It's different, but it's beginning to feel good, having some flexibility and freedom.

(Ok, here it is . . .)

What's the worst that can happen?
A: Well, I wouldn't leave without knowing I could get *some* work, but I might not do very well for the first year. So I need some savings to tide me over. And my dad might lend me £10,000. I might not enjoy it or not get the quality of work. But I'd probably learn a lot, about myself as well as my work, and get ideas. And I'm sure I could get back into employment if I decided it wasn't for me.

So what has Carol done here in her self-coaching session? She has realised that information is vital and she has thought about where she can go for that information. She has begun to create a picture for herself of where she might work and what she might be doing, and the kind of lifestyle she might have. She has considered the possibility that potential competitors might be helpful to her. She will consider alternative scenarios such as getting a new job to develop her experience and CV and gaining new qualifications, delaying her launch for a year or more. And armed with this information she has gained a new, optimistic perspective (glass half full rather than glass half empty).

Might you fear success?

There may be other, more complex, reasons for procrastination, such as fear of or guilt from success. Perhaps there is someone close to you who would be disapproving or jealous of your achievement. Or you just can't see yourself as a responsible business person, with good money or getting attention.

Self-defeating beliefs (like Carol's above) are an emotional trait recognised in cognitive behavioural therapy. If you experience this, you need to address these thoughts, working them through in whatever way suits you and your pocket. There are self-help books, coaches and therapists who can help you do this.

Look at risk

Another aspect of fear is far more useful in business: caution. Carol challenged her beliefs, the gremlins on her shoulder. But not all gremlins are wrong! An intrinsic part of planning is risk analysis, which not many self-employed people do. Essentially, the more there is to lose, the more important is risk analysis. If you are seeking outside finance, other people will want to know the risk to their money as well.

Risk analysis is an integral part of the insurance industry. You don't have to lie awake at night worrying about a client tripping over your carpet and smashing the only version of their invention that has taken five years to complete. The insurer has calculated that risk in developing its public liability product (although you might still want to make sure your carpet edges are safely secured).

❛ *The only risk was £100. I am not good at taking risks, especially with money.* ❜

Lisa Cole, Lactivist

A simple (non-numerical) risk analysis deploys focused common sense and a good bit of research. It comes back to our 'what if' questions and scenario planning.

TRY THIS

Factors	Consider	How to mitigate/protect
The market	Is there a demand for my product/service; who else is in it, at what price?	Carry out market research
Recession	Is this going to affect the business?	Read; get advice; talk to clients and others in the market
The product/service	Can I provide this to the required quality?	Check premises; your costs and expertise
Weather	How might adverse weather affect you?	Insurance; secure premises/ storage facilities
Computer	Data loss; loss of files	Ensure computer security and backup
Family and personal	Illness, breakup	What support do you have? Can anyone else step in?
Despite all your wonderful planning, something turns out different	A supplier doesn't deliver; a client changes their mind...	Build in flexibility; 'rainy day' cash; cancellation insurance

Any of this kind of analysis will be good for your business plan – the bank manager will be really impressed!

❝ I researched the areas we planned to operate in and found that there was a lot more competition than I had at first thought. It took longer than anticipated to finalise the area where the magazine would be distributed but at the time of starting we were unopposed, which was a big help. I canvassed local businesses face to face and asked them their thoughts, whether they would advertise and what they would want to pay etc. ❞

Kristina Thomas, Sussex Local Magazine

But before you rush off to Google 'risk analysis', get the handbook, take the qualification: don't panic! A conversation with your insurance broker or bank manager can get you up to speed. See the Appendix section for a useful booklet.

CHAPTER FOUR

WILL IT WORK?
RESEARCHING THE MARKET

Advisers will tell you: the weakest area in business startup is research. Why?

- I'm good at this/fancy having a go.
- I know I can do it this way.
- I'd be better than this lot and they're doing alright.
- I've got a bit of money behind me, I can't lose.
- I'm really excited, so let's get going!

What are your thoughts on research?

You'll see in some of our case studies and comments how research helps – and where lack of it jeopardises the business. There really is only one piece of advice – DO IT! Do some, any amount, even if you don't have a budget to hire a research company. The more you know about your market and your prospects in it, the greater your chances of success.

Types of research
- Talk to people.
- Get stats and figures.
- Who is the competition?
- Visit, sample.
- Find potential clients, customers – have a questionnaire, interview them.
- Test your ideas or product.

So let's go!

Talk to people

Who is in your (target) marketplace? If you plan to set up in your area of expertise, you have a head start. You know the suppliers and purchasers, the industry or professional groups and possibly the prices/fees.

A market is typically made up of suppliers, purchasers, advisers, possibly recruiters and sometimes observers like researchers and journalists.

Suppliers

You may not be able to talk to suppliers, who would become your competitors, but you can get information on them. You could be crafty and make some enquiries before you leave your job, perhaps as a potential purchaser. However, if it's a very close-knit business, think carefully before you go too far. Competitors are inevitable, enemies are unwanted. Websites give a certain amount of information.

Purchasers

Talk to purchasers. Can you send a questionnaire or interview a few? Find out what they want and whether there is unmet demand, a gap. Tap as many contacts as you can. Could you have a discussion with your employer (some can be grown-up about this) to see what they would think of hiring you as a contractor or supplier?

Advisers

Advisers include management or other consultants, lawyers and accountants. Do they have reports or papers online? Can you attend any seminars (for free)? Is there a friendly one who can talk about the marketplace? In a few clicks you can find free guides (albeit you might have to give them your email address).

Recruiters

Recruiters really know the marketplace and they are sometimes keen to have good freelancers/contractors on their books. If your employer is paranoid, it might be best to avoid their favourite recruiters; if you left under a cloud, a recruiter used by your employer would be loath to take you on their books. Let's hope you don't work for such a dominant company that there are no recruiters left untouched. Ask them about the freelance market, the supply of work, who they would put on their books, the likelihood of you getting work and what kind, and what rates.

Remember, if you end up working for only one agency, you may be considered to be an employee of that agency, even if you have different jobs. Ask them about their pay and tax policy.

Market commentators

Look for research reports, journals and industry magazines for information and ideas. Many are online nowadays. Are there any conferences or exhibitions you can attend?

Stats and information

What information would be useful to you? You may want to know how much a market is worth; whether spending on your skill area is increasing; how big the freelance or outsourced sector is; certainly the rates of pay. This is where the internet search comes into its own (although you can still be led down many blind alleys).

Useful sources of information

- Government stats.
- Market and business data (such as Mintel Reports).
- Professional associations.
- Industry associations.
- Chambers of Commerce.
- Company information.
- Recruitment reports (such as salary surveys).
- Websites for freelancers (see Reference section).

TRY THIS

Whatever industry or sector you plan to go into, search for research reports and statistics. Compile your own report asking:

▶ What kind of market share or sales should I set out to get?
▶ How big a player would I be?
▶ Is the market dominated by a few big companies?
▶ Who would be my competitors?
▶ What price/fees should I set?

Research the competition

Go undercover

This is where your endeavours could get murky...Can you enlist a colleague who is already a purchaser (or could pretend to be one) and ask them to call competitors and get information? Look at their websites. Network. It may be a collegiate type of industry where they don't mind sharing information. They may have so much work they could sub-contract some to you, although it's unlikely they would pay as well as working direct.

Visit, sample

If you are going into a sector where premises are required, or a physical product is produced, can you visit and try out, mystery shopper style? Try a fitness session with a personal trainer, a beauty session, wardrobe consultation. If you pay, it's perfectly honest, but don't give the game away by asking 101 questions! Be subtle about it.

Test your ideas or product

In the end, the proof is in the pudding. All the big consumer companies test their products on potential customers and so can you. You could offer a demonstration, a couple of free hours of your service, arrange to send samples of your work to a specific person and then follow up for feedback. Make sure you get honest responses and act on negative feedback. Improve your offering.

If you have a sizeable budget, you can commission market research by a specialist agency. Be very clear in your brief, what you will get from the agency and how you will be able to use that information. At the freelance level, though, there is no replacement for getting down and dirty. Often when you are doing research you are also, subtly, selling. And if you put together a good questionnaire, you could come out with some original market data that you could use for public relations purposes.

Put a time limit on it

Lastly, don't take too long with your research. Market data changes and even in six months you could be acting on old information. Also, you may not be the only person planning to do what you want to do, and the more you talk about your plans, the more they can be leaked and copied. Make a timetable for the research and a timeframe for assessing it.

Allow yourself time for setting up

CASE STUDY

Pearce Marketing, established and run by Emma Pearce
www.pearcemarketing.co.uk
Business: Marketing planning and outsourced/interim marketing services for small and mid-sized businesses

Emma began Pearce Marketing in September 2008, not the easiest time to launch a new business as the recession was getting under way. She also launched in what many would find distressing circumstances. She was made redundant the day she returned to work from nine months' maternity leave, as she describes:

'I had been on the senior management team of my employer for four years in a marketing role and have got 15 years' marketing work behind me locally, nationally and internationally. I had my first child and returned to work and by lunchtime that day I had been made redundant. It was a huge shock. However the recession hit my employer hard.'

What did that mean for her launch?
'When I set up I was feeling a bit on the back foot. I had not intended to set up my own business at that time. My confidence had taken quite a knock with the shock of redundancy; plus, I had been out of the business networking circuit and workplace for nine months.

But with the recession digging its heels in, there weren't many job options, particularly as I was a first time mum returning to work. Plus, I had made a decision to work part time, initially. My needs were to work more locally, to have a decent income to pay the mortgage and to keep doing good quality senior level marketing work. I liked the idea of running my own business but I had never got close to doing it before. I was excited, but concerned.

I did have a slight reprieve financially as I had my mortgage holiday (for my maternity period) running for another three months and I had a couple of thousand pounds to help start up the business. But the need was to get back earning, which meant I didn't have time to delay. So I got on with things.

And my launch went well with an immediate client, due to good contacts and a good track record.'

What planning did she do?
'Due to the haste, I didn't do a full business plan before launching the business (against my own advice). I would always recommend doing market research and a business plan, but as my business had its first customer, I didn't have the time! I had, however, done some research on

pricing before I won my first client and met with business advisers and contacts to talk through ideas and plans.'

What else helped?

'My husband, family and a couple of respected business contacts gave me encouragement to set up the company. Also, within the first two months I did a presentation at a confidential networking group to get feedback on how to best approach and succeed as a marketing consultant. I also got feedback on my logo and designs – it was like a focus group. Since then, though, I have investigated competitors and made an effort to meet some of them. In fact, I've done work for one of them as a marketing associate.

In addition, I have worked with a consultant as part of a package within a networking group membership. I looked at what I should be doing to develop the business and I've put that into practice. I didn't change my original ideas but I have fine-tuned them. I've also planned and delivered my own marketing activities including a website, writing articles, setting up email marketing and joining new business networks.

Since then, business has been steady. Four years of local networking has paid off: I've helped a company prepare a marketing plan and have an ongoing contract delivering various marketing activities for them. Overall, clients range from one-person-bands to a company with a turnover of £10m+.'

What are the main challenges?

'There is so much to do to set up a business and even once you are up and running at a simple level, there is always more development work. The main issue is balancing time for fee earning work with trying to win new business and coping with all the admin, billing and marketing work that needs to be done too. I intended to work three days per week and look after my daughter for the other two. However, I have needed to work more than that. This is partly because I have been busier than expected (a good problem really) but also because more time is required to run a business than you first imagine. I work some evenings and often while my daughter naps on the days I am with her. It is also a challenge for my husband (who is not self employed) to understand the essential demands on my time because I can be a bit of a workaholic!'

What was key to her getting through the launch period?
'The best thing I did was to get feedback from business peers and contacts at the start. It gives you confidence and meaningful information to go in the right direction. I met face to face, sent them drafts of my web copy, found out about new networks to join and asked about my competitors. Networking is vital for my type of business. It is the main marketing/lead generation source.'

CHAPTER FIVE

WILL IT WORK?
YOUR PERSONALITY TRAITS

As we are in realistic (if not pessimistic) mode in this section, let's consider the personal demands of working for yourself. Do you have the romantic notion: no more boss; free to walk the dog in the day; pay less tax? Here are some real truths and the personality traits or tactics that can tackle them:

Some truths	Dependent upon:
Isolation at home	Being okay with own company
Have to keep hustling for work	A thick skin
Don't get work	Resilience
Have to keep your own books	A practical streak
Yes, you still have to pay tax!	Getting a good accountant
Lots of meetings and no earning while you are travelling (inefficient use of time)	Planning or pricing right
Lower-grade work as temp	Sticking to your plan and holding out
Being at the beck and call of clients	Gaining more authority and being patient
Competitors undercut price	Market data and flexibility
Late payment	Financial planning and chasing
Having to chase or sue for payment	A serious attitude to money from the start
Can't say 'No', so working 24/7	A serious attitude to yourself
Too many distractions	A rethink?
Too early in your career	Waiting a while?

You could probably think of more as you develop your particular working situation and put it against your personality and circumstances.

TRY THIS

Personality test

1. Do you smile at people you don't know in the street? Yes/No
2. If you see a recently bereaved acquaintance, do you go up and talk to her? Yes/No
3. Can you manage without life's luxuries? Yes/No
4. Can you pick yourself up if things go wrong? Yes/No
5. Do you embrace change? Yes/No
6. Can you say 'No' if a friend calls for a coffee? Yes/No
7. Are you comfortable addressing a group of people? Yes/No
8. Do you generally roll up your sleeves and muck in? Yes/No
9. Do you believe compromise is essential in an argument? Yes/No
10. Have you ever gone for a walk not knowing where you are going? Yes/No
11. Do you feel guilty if you miss the school sports day? Yes/No
12. Do you get upset if people reject your ideas? Yes/No
13. Is your motto, 'Your job should be fun'? Yes/No
14. Is your social life sacrosanct? Yes/No
15. Are you good at blaming other people? Yes/No
16. Does asking for money make you feel uncomfortable? Yes/No
17. Do you mostly give in to people in an argument? Yes/No
18. Are you a worrier? Yes/No
19. Do you believe being in debt is a bad thing? Yes/No
20. Everything in life is down to fate. Do you agree? Yes/No

Questions 1–10: Score 2 for every yes, 1 for every no
Questions 11–20: Score 1 for every yes, 2 for every no

Your score

20–30 You need to really question whether going into business is right for you. Here's some of the things you should reflect on: giving up time and money; taking risk without becoming over stressed; being thick skinned; being comfortable with people in pressured situations; being matter-of-fact about money.

30–40 You have an outlook that could suit going into business. You know you need to be friendly and confident with people on both formal and personal levels; you are prepared to graft and you can cope with risk and uncertainty.

Personality traits

You need to be honest about your strengths and weaknesses, and your little foibles. There are likely to be some character traits that will have to change if you work for yourself (whether at home, in outside premises or in a corporate environment).

Laziness is the big one. It won't get you far even in employment, but perhaps someone else's big stick keeps you going. Or maybe you can get away with a low output at work. When you are out on your own, there is no crutch. If no one else is pushing you, how efficient will you be? Clients won't accept missed deadlines; customers won't chase you. And what will drive you to chase business anyway?

Self discipline is essential and you need to think carefully if you are not (in the jargon) a self-starter, good at time keeping, productive and focused (no one will pay you to update your Facebook profile or book a holiday). And if money is the *only* motivator, you are unlikely to produce a business based on excellence, cutting-edge results and with growth potential.

Confidence and **communication skills** are vital in most businesses. You don't have to be the life and soul of the party but you need to be able to meet and greet strangers, make eye contact, listen and respond confidently. In addition, you need to sell subtly, make small talk and possibly address an audience. No wonder there are so many speaking courses around!

You should be friendly and inquisitive – every customer or client is your next piece of market research. You can find out what they want in a casual conversation. At any level of business we are more likely to buy from people we like and trust. So, whether you are extrovert or introvert, you have to develop the persona that fits your particular market.

Another important trait is being **thick skinned**. The small business (female- or male-run) has long complained how badly treated it is by the big corporations. And in the consumer sector you may have to deal with all kinds of abuse. Unless you are very lucky, you will, at some point, need to cold sell.

TRY THIS

Can you hack any of this? How does it make you feel?

► Getting the cold shoulder from the telephonist.
► Getting through to your target who is then rude to you.
► People lying to you to get rid of you.
► People leading you on and wasting your time.
► Turning up for a meeting on time and being kept waiting for hours.
► Turning up for a meeting to be told the appointment isn't in the diary (and your target is out).
► Having your presentation pulled apart.
► Sending samples and getting no reply.
► Discovering you are pitching to someone who has no authority to purchase.
► People haggling over your rates or prices.
► Being told 'We'll get back to you' and then they don't.
► People nit-picking with your work.
► People rejecting your work or saying it doesn't follow the brief.
► People rejecting your work and later presenting it as their own.
► People copying your designs.
► Delivering a great project and not having it used.
► People arguing over your bill or not paying.
► Theft or fraud.

How thick is your skin now – six inches? We all take knocks at work and in our personal life, but somehow when we set up in business there can be so many more. This is your cherished business, it's you, and it's difficult not to take things personally. There are a number of reasons for this and in addition to developing defence mechanisms, there are some practical things you can build in.

Minimise the knocks (business to business)

Make introductions

In a new business you have to hustle; but remember, people at work get a lot of unsolicited calls so businesses will try and weed them out, politely or otherwise. Can you get through to people by networking or introduction instead? Can you attend an exhibition or conference, give a talk or take exhibition space? It's more acceptable to hustle in these circumstances.

Research

Do your research properly and make sure you are talking to the right person and that they are serious about what you are offering. Email confirmation of the meeting; cc their line manager if you have had dealings with them as well.

Put it in writing

There will always be people who argue over your work or bill. Be very clear, use terms of business (how you work) plus a confirming letter: what you have agreed to deliver (with description or specs), by when and at what price. Stand firm when you know you have delivered. Get advice on your ownership (intellectual property) and copyright where you can. As a last resort, can you go over their head to their line manager?

Be serious about money

Find out your clients' payment processes. Sometimes you can chase the finance department for payment and they get things moving. Take prompt payment seriously.

Look after yourself

Look at your security aspects – computer, trading, premises, access to the public, employees. Get advice from the appropriate source (see Appendix).

The last major trait is **self image**. Women are often less confident than men when setting up in business. Most of us want to be nice (quite rightly too!). But you won't get very far if you let people walk all over you. You need to take yourself and your venture seriously, otherwise people will take advantage and jeopardise your success.

Do business with confidence

- Do your market research properly so you know what your competitors charge, what they are delivering and where your product/service stands out. Politely respond to objections that you know are inaccurate.

- Most people will negotiate hard, even try it on, before they get to know you. Learn to pick the clients who will respect you, and dump the clients who will never make you money. Learn to put across your product or service in terms of value.

- Make sure your literature or presentation is factually accurate and your assertions can be backed up so you can stand up to challenges when they arise.

■ Be confident about what you are selling and how good you are. Take an assertiveness course if needed. Rehearse meetings and presentations.

■ Be prepared to walk away; don't hang around with people who don't value your work.

■ It's corny, but if you need to, make a huge poster saying 'I'M WORTH IT!' Hang it in front of your desk with your photo on!

CHAPTER SIX

THE SERIOUS STUFF: SELF EMPLOYMENT

Once your business ideas begin to take shape, you need to give thought to the regulatory aspects of trading and self employment. We can't cover every minutia here, and some things will change, especially when a government changes (so please check all information). Here you will get an overview and pointers for more information. There is a great deal of advice around, not least from Business Link online, specialist books and banks' and advisers' websites. See the Appendix for more details.

It's also important that you do your own research for your particular circumstances. This is general information, relevant to most self-employed situations. Later, in Part Four, we'll look at different businesses and circumstances.

Make sure it's legal

You do not need a lawyer to set you up in business, but they might help. At its simplest, you have to decide on your status – sole trader, partnership or limited company and you must ensure this is all set up correctly tax wise.

Sole trader
Sole trader is the simplest way of trading and you must register within three months of setting up. You will be self employed and you must file your annual tax returns via self assessment. You do not have limited liability so should look into what insurance suits your needs. As a self-employed person, you pay minimal National Insurance contributions so, depending on your employment history, you may not qualify for benefits, including maternity benefit. You should also consider some kind of pension plan for yourself.

Partnership
Partnership status is for two or more people going into business together. You should get tax and legal advice as to whether this suits you. Some professional businesses, such as lawyers and accountants, are currently required to be partnerships. There is also a more recent structure, limited liability partnership.

As the name says, this limits each partner's liability to the amount invested or guaranteed.

Limited company

Limited company is popular because of the word 'limited'. However, directors have liability so don't be fooled into thinking you can walk away from debts or other liabilities (not that you would, of course). You register your company with Companies House. You would be a director and an employee so therefore eligible for benefits, should you need them, and you should consider a personal or company pension scheme.

Social enterprises

These operate principally with social objectives and profit is mostly ploughed back in (see Chapter 27). They can take different formal structures (such as companies limited by guarantees or shares, or industrial and provident societies). You should get legal or financial advice to determine your personal status.

Contractual relationships

Some women take on franchises and direct selling agencies (see Chapter 27). You'll need to sort out your tax and legal status, depending on your income and circumstances.

When can a lawyer help?

If your business grows, there are many times when legal advice will be useful or necessary.

> *Advice on company structure and drawing up proper legal agreements*
> *– Renting or buying business property*
> *– Dealing with regulations (some sector specific)*
> *– Contract terms with suppliers and customers*
> *– Protecting intellectual property (business ideas)*
> *– Raising finance*
> *– Debt control*
> *– Franchising*
> *– Employment law.*

Business Link website, *Practical Advice for Business*

Make sure you use a commercial lawyer, not your local high street solicitor who may take you on, but really deals only with probate, conveyancing and divorce. Ask for a fixed fee and talk to the person you will deal with most; make sure you get on with them. A law firm will provide you with advice, but, compared with your accountant, your relationship with a lawyer is more likely to be transactional than ongoing. All the same, make sure you are on the seminar mailing list!

Get clued up on finances

It's a good idea to do some financial planning before you launch, even if it's just a simple spreadsheet (see Chapter 16). You can get help with this from your bank adviser or an accountant. Check if they charge for this.

Other tips on finance for the self employed

- Open a business account; it will keep your work finances separate from your personal ones (even though you will have to pay charges). You could be invited to business seminars and networking events in your area.

- You must keep all your receipts and bank statements, and organise your invoices. Even if you don't do your own accounts (profit and loss, and balance sheet), at least do your figures yourself (cash book). Keep a record of payments into and out of your account. *Always* know how your cash flow is going. That way you will keep a watch on how the business is doing and understand it much better.

- Inform the Inland Revenue when you start trading.

- If you prefer to, you can hire a bookkeeper to record transactions (from your cash book). They can also prepare VAT returns, if you are registered, and payroll if you employ anyone.

- An accountant can prepare your annual accounts and your tax return, if you don't want to do these yourself (see box below).

 ❛ *Self-employed sole traders and most partnerships don't need to create a formal profit and loss account – the information they complete on the self-assessment tax return form amounts to the same thing. However, there are key benefits to producing formal accounts. If you are looking to grow your business, or need a loan or mortgage, for example, most institutions will ask to see three years' accounts.* ❜
Business Link website, *Practical Advice for Business*

A few more facts

A sole trader pays tax in arrears based on the tax return (so you have to be good at saving!). An accountant can often save you their fee or more with their tax advice. They will also keep you disciplined to get your tax return in on time (it's staggering how many people file late and get fined). If your turnover goes above the limit (and is growing) then you must register for VAT, whether as a sole trader or limited company. A sole trader can also employ people. Be warned, some agencies and companies do not do business with sole traders.

A limited company

If you launch as a limited company, you must file audited accounts with Companies House. As a director you will also be an employee and taxed on a PAYE basis. An accountant can advise you on matters such as shares, salary and pensions.

Choosing an accountant

- A local bookkeeper can be cheaper than using an accountant to do your books.

- Choose a small firm of accountants and don't be nervous about asking their fees. They usually have a fixed fee for small and start-up clients.

- Ask how much start-up advice you can expect to get. Talk to the person who would be your accountant and see how savvy they are. You want to get on with this person as they can be a great help.

- Does the firm have free client seminars, a good newsletter, useful website offering advice?

- Are they tapped into the local economy, so could make introductions?

Other sources of support

- With the demise of the advice element of Business Link, look out for new agencies taking on this role.

- A good coach can be both guide and mentor and can help you find the inspiration and solutions to developing your business.

- Networks, both mixed and women only, are invaluable and provide advice, training, support, contacts, suppliers, customers and friends.

Summary checklist: Getting started

✓ Examine your motivation for working for yourself.
✓ Think about the role and importance of money in your life.
✓ Present your business in a professional way.
✓ Plan how your work will fit in with your lifestyle.
✓ Get the right team of suppliers around you.
✓ Face up to fear and procrastination.
✓ Analyse potential risks to your business.
✓ Conduct solid market research.
✓ Consider your personality traits and preferences.
✓ Build up your defence mechanisms.
✓ Set up your legal status.
✓ Know when a lawyer or accountant can help.
✓ Look for support when you need it: don't struggle alone.

Part 2:
The Expert

Introduction

Many women work for themselves because they have experience in an industry or vocation that they can exploit. Sectors such as IT, journalism, public relations, production management, admin, medical, HR and finance all hire freelancers, contractors or interims (temporary management posts). This can be for projects, covering maternity leave or other resourcing needs. They may hire you for a few days a month (such as on a retainer) or full time on a temporary basis. Interim management and other forms of outplaced work have been big growth industries in the past few years.

As well as offering more flexibility (sometimes) it can be an opportunity to increase your income, compared with being employed. You may also be able to control the direction of your career more. And it could offer a stepping stone to developing a bigger business; for instance through setting up an agency, employing others in your field.

There is great variation between industries in terms of professional requirements, such as:

- qualifications
- licensing or accreditation
- ethical boundaries
- insurance
- health and safety.

If you are a qualified professional, you should do your research and contact your professional body to ensure you are operating legally and ethically. This Part now looks at the general aspects which cover most vocations.

CHAPTER SEVEN

THE NUTS AND BOLTS OF FREELANCING

You can go freelance or become a contractor at any time in your life, but most successful contractors will have gained some training and experience in the corporate environment. However, this is less of a hard-and-fast rule today than a generation ago (see Chapter 26).

TRY THIS

Write down the advantages and disadvantages of going freelance for you:

Advantages	Disadvantages
Can give you flexibility to develop a second career, write a book, look after family.	You may have to cope with periods of insecurity concerning work and earnings.
Greater earnings potential than in employment; tax advantages too.	If sole trader, you have to look after own tax affairs and you MUST save to pay taxes twice a year.
Plan the work (and income) right and you can take longer holidays!	The work isn't usually handed to you on a plate, so you have to market yourself regularly.
If you have the right experience you can develop a niche of cutting edge work.	You may get only the basic stuff that needs plodding through.
You could build a personal reputation if you work for yourself.	You will probably have to fund your own training and other benefits.
Variety of work, clients and workplace settings.	You must sort out your own insurances, pension, etc.
The contractor can enjoy a better status within an organisation than the in-house equivalent.	Even if you are on site, it can be isolating; you won't be one of 'the team'.

Talk tax

Essentially, you cannot go freelance and just work for one 'client' as Revenue and Customs (HMRC) will not consider you to be self employed. So you can't leave your company one evening as an employee and walk back in the next morning, with your photos, coffee mug and email address all where they were, and say you are a contractor. This was made official by a law called IR35, which took effect in 2000, and a lot of contractors, particularly in the IT field, were scooped into the PAYE (taxed as an employee) net. It was pretty controversial at the time.

You will have to prove to HMRC that you are genuinely self employed, which can be difficult if you are just starting. Employers, too, need to be convinced, as they do not want the tax man claiming unpaid tax from them if you do a runner (which, of course, you won't!) See the Appendix and talk to HMRC.

Once you have been given the okay to be self employed, congratulations, you are set up working for yourself! You could set up as a limited company if you prefer (see Chapter 6). Check the requirements for this with Companies House or get professional help.

Is an interim self employed?

If you are contracted to a recruitment or supply agency and all your work comes through the agency, you may well be an employee of that agency. If so, they will take off tax and National Insurance. So, technically, you are not freelance even if you work in different workplaces or for different people. One test by HMRC is where you work and what hours. For instance, if you work Mondays to Wednesdays in one company and Thursdays and Fridays in another, you could be classed as part time (employed) for each. Other tests include who controls your work and whether you have to follow an employer's instructions. So again, check before you set up (see Appendix).

What could you earn?

How much you earn will depend upon:

- the state of the market (boom or bust?)
- your level of experience and thus fees
- the supply of competitors (over supply can drive down rates)

■ how many (paid) hours you work (see time sheets below)
■ how good a negotiator you are.

You need to do good research (see Chapter 4) and talk to lots of people. If your work will come through agencies, these are the people to see. They will be quite honest about whether they can find work for you and at what rate.

If you are going to work directly for clients then you have to do competitor research to find out what kind of livings are being made by those already there. Do you have an edge on them – qualifications, experience, skills etc.? Look at their websites, ask professional associations (who might also run training on working for yourself). Try to talk to potential clients.

Good research before you launch will help you get your sales pitch right as well because you will be addressing what they need. For instance, if you want to become an interim human resources (HR) consultant and businesses are deep in redundancy rounds, you won't want to emphasise your search and selection skills so much as your 'outplacement' handling.

Budget for the early years

How can you gauge the state of the market and whether you will be successful? Outside of boom times – and we are supposedly going to be outside of a boom time for a few years yet – your research and financial planning are vital. Some people are lucky to have one or two clients lined up when they launch, often their existing employer as one. Otherwise, it's down to your attitude to risk and how long you can manage financially before you start earning. As a general rule you will take at least two years to earn the kind of money you would like. Holidays are over rated, anyway!

It is essential to keep a tight rein on costs, especially marketing costs (see Chapter 11). Much of the freelance world depends on word-of-mouth, so don't get sucked into expensive directory listings or exhibition stands unless you know they work.

' *I take a cautious approach to risk. I have invested only what I can afford to lose and I am already recouping some of that investment. I have also kept my eye on the interim management market and kept my contacts, so if the worst came to the worst I can earn money whilst my business is establishing itself.* '

Emma Lodge, Director, Balance Accounting Solutions

Plan your finances

In your financial planning (see Chapter 16) you can put in a range of incomes in different scenarios: a pessimistic one through to (mildly) optimistic. Put in your costs and you can see whether you make a profit. Then pick yourself up from the floor and halve the costs – you'll feel better!

Seriously, don't put in figures just to get a good end result. If in Year 1 you make a loss – which is to be expected – you can plan for a loan. We'll talk later on about our attitude to borrowing money, but don't let your business fail for lack of start-up finance. Be realistic with your forecasts and make sure you can live while your income builds up.

Is a recession good for the self employed?

A recession doesn't necessarily mean an increase in contract work. Some businesses will cut projects and non-staff posts first, while others need freelancers to fill gaps left by redundancy programmes. As we pull out of recession, they may prefer interims or consultants before they have the confidence to recruit full time employees again. So there could be opportunities as we go through the second decade of the century; it depends on your sector or expertise.

❛ *I knew I had a strong enough network of contacts and reputation so I was fairly sure that it would go ok. I also knew that there were a lot of companies out there who had made their marketing people redundant but still needed to market their businesses, and also companies who couldn't afford a chartered marketer on their payroll.* ❜

Corinne McLavy, Director, Zero3 Marketing

❛ *Some of my friends and family thought I should stop and get a job, especially with the impending recession. But I felt that this would be a great time for my business, and I have been proved right. My quarterly sales this financial year have exceeded my annual sales of the previous year.* ❜

Karen Purves, Centre for Effective Marketing

Starting up in a recession, keeping your costs and prices keen, can be a successful strategy. That's not to ignore the fact, though, that many businesses have been damaged by the deep recession suffered towards the end of the decade.

❛ *The very last line of the SWOT analysis of my business plan talked about the possibility of a recession. And then I launched the business just as all the banks were going bust! I think it has affected the business quite a lot (like all retailers and a lot of green businesses too); but I think consumers are starting to shop again. Green consumers have strong core values and they want to buy products they believe in: they may buy less but they do stay loyal to brands and products that they trust.* ❜

Tabitha Harman, Mimimyne

Work out your rates/fees

In this section we are talking about an individual selling their services by time, the most common way freelancers are paid. That means earnings will be the number of hours/days you intend to work (or can get work for) multiplied by the hourly/daily rate. You might plan to work three days a week but if you can't get your desired rate then you won't earn what you want. Can you increase your hours or your rate? Let's look at each scenario.

Payment through a recruitment agency

If you work through an agency they will give you a rate for the job they are putting you up for, likely to be a daily rate. You may have some leeway for negotiation, but the end client is likely to have a fixed rate for that job. If you want more, you might price yourself out of the job, so it will depend on how much you need/want the job. When you begin you may not yet have the reputation to be able to charge a premium. Also, the complex work or projects could be put on hold in a downturn.

The agency will establish your tax status with you when they enrol you, so your money from the agency, at the end of the week, will either be gross or net of tax and National Insurance.

Payment direct from the client

Here you could charge nearer the rates that the agency charges the clients, although it might be an advantage to undercut them. And you know the rates, because you have done your research, haven't you?

You'll therefore earn more but you'll have to do your own marketing to find and get known to clients. Clients often prefer using an agency which does the vetting for them, ignoring the fact that they could hire someone direct for less. And if a client hires several freelancers through the same agency, timesheets and billing are streamlined.

How do you know what to charge?

Clients may hire you for a project – work with an end time, fixed budget and clear desired outcomes. So they will want to negotiate a fixed fee with you. Most likely you'll need to quote for the job on the basis of how long it is likely to take you (plus any costs you incur). This is difficult when you are starting up. You will want to make your best efforts, particularly if it's the first job for that client; but if it takes you twice as long as you estimated, you will earn half the rate you wanted.

Worse, you won't have that time to work for other clients to make up the earnings. Quoting is a difficulty in any industry, and until you become established you won't be sure how long a job will take you. That's the risk of retainer work – charging a fixed fee (retainer) based on, say, three days a month. If the client keeps giving you work to do and it takes four, even five days, what do you do?

Negotiation skills for fixed fee work

Here are some tips (based on bitter experience):

When you first interview or pitch for the work, ask how flexible they are on budget, should your time overrun.

You will have to bring the conversation round to a negotiation – they aren't going to suggest paying you more!

Introduce the subject of work levels and say you need to discuss how overworking can be tackled.

Give them the option of having a contingency to pay for overtime, or holding back on work (perhaps until the next month).

Tell them you would like to review the account in six months' time.

It's better to sit down and discuss fees calmly than having to say every month, 'You've used up your fees!'

On a fixed fee project, you won't be able to ask for more at the end unless you build in conditions.

For instance, if the client delayed, incurring more of your time. If you've under-quoted for the job, you could try asking for more, but otherwise see it as a learning curve.

Above all, take your business seriously, even if your client doesn't.

If you work on site for a fixed number of hours and there is a late working culture, don't get dragged into it.

Many clients want something for nothing and you are working for nothing if you go over time. Either renegotiate or ditch the client after that job.

Staff may get overtime, you don't. The odd hour or so extra as a goodwill gesture may not hurt but if it goes on, negotiate extra. Why should you work for nothing just because you are self employed?

❝ *I would normally meet a client for an initial chat and then write a proposal for them to review. The costs within a proposal are based on a daily rate. The day rate is typically set by me within my proposal; however, it is possible that a client will want to negotiate my rates.* ❞

Emma Pearce, Pearce Marketing Consultants

Death by timesheet

Welcome to the world of the timesheet. It's irritating and easy to forget, but if you work on an hourly or daily rate, the timesheet must go everywhere with you. It gives you the only means of working out your efficiency and therefore what rate you are achieving.

❝ *When I work from home on the client projects I continue to work at the daily rate set in the proposal. The price is for my time wherever I work. I do, however, only charge them for the time I spend – so if I only needed to work on something for four hours, I would charge pro rata. I keep time sheets for each client ready for billing at the end of each month.* ❞

Emma Pearce, Pearce Marketing Consultants

It may sound easy, especially if you work on site for full days, but what if:

■ you work in three locations for two different clients, some full days and some half days?

■ you fill out your timesheets at the end of the month – on the 27th you lose your diary?

■ you are working on three projects for different clients, a few hours daily for each; you complete your timesheets at the end of the day, but regularly forget and have to do them the next morning?

■ you have your timesheets on paper, scribbling every block of two or three hours; you spill coffee on your pad of 30 completed timesheets?

Ok, that's enough! You've probably got the message!

■ Complete them for each block of work, before you move on to another client or take a break.

■ Finalise them at the end of each day.

■ Note them on paper and then put them on your computer as well. That week, if not that day.

■ Total them for the month and compare them with the estimated hours –what you need to work to get your day rate.

■ There are timesheet packages you can buy, although for one person they may not be cost effective.

You will probably take a few months to settle and to build up efficiency, so accept overworking to begin with. Note what areas of work or which accounts are taking longer and think of ways to speed up.

TRY THIS
Compile your own timesheet

A timesheet can be quite simple to do provided you can create a table. It requires your making a note of the time when you begin and end a task, or enter and leave the client's premises. A daily timesheet (three clients) might look like the example on the opposite page.

Example timesheet – daily

Day/time	Client A (hours)	Client B	Client C
Monday 9–10.30 10.30–4.30 (1 hour break) 5–6.30	1.5	5	1.5
Tuesday 10–12 12–2 (Break) 2–5	2	3	
Wednesday 11–2 2–4		2	3
Thursday 9–1 1–2 (Break) 2–5	4 Break 3		
Friday 9–11 11–12.30 2–3.30 (Break) 3.30–5 5–6	2 1.5	 1	1.5
Total for week	A: 14 hours	B: 11	C: 6

Alternatively, you might have one sheet per client and give more detail of the tasks done. Such a breakdown of your work is often required by the client.

Client A – Monday		
9–11	Telephone interviews	2
11–12	Research	1
12–1.30	Break	
1.30–4	Research	2.5
4–5.30	Report writing	1.5
Total		7

Billing and invoicing

If you are charging open ended by time – quite rare, these days – you will have an accurate and accountable system for billing. You should summarise the times on the invoice or, if the client wants, attach the timesheet (or send it to the client and the invoice to accounts, depending on their requirements).

If you are working by fixed fee, the time probably won't be of interest to the client, so the timesheet is to let you know how efficient you are being. You will invoice the client for the fee, monthly or for whatever time period agreed. State the work done, by title (e.g., Stage 3 of Project). Again, find out from the client what reporting and accountability they need. Sometimes you can invoice in advance, sometimes not.

Add disbursements (your costs on behalf of the client) according to your agreement. Add VAT if you are VAT-registered. And try not to make mistakes: these mess up your books and if in the client's favour, they may not point them out to you! Don't do billing late at night or after a glass of wine!

Put your payment terms in your Terms of Business. Thirty days is normal and be tough on chasing up. Find the person in accounts to chase and try to avoid regular payment niggles with your client contact (unless they are really bad).

There are a few websites devoted to freelancing. The quality of work is variable and they aren't aimed at the qualified professional, but they offer lots of tips on setting up, accounting and so on. See the Appendix.

CHAPTER EIGHT

WHERE WILL YOU WORK?

Most likely your workplace will be determined by the client. Some lucky freelancers can alternate home and client workplace, getting the best of both worlds. Home is simple and cheap but may not be practical. Even if you have a room that will serve as an office it can be difficult keeping equipment, client records and other materials away from young children. You may have to build in the cost of a small office or workshop, perhaps sharing with others. See 'Commercial property' in the Appendix.

Pros and cons: Working from home

Weigh up the pros and cons of each scenario, for you.

Pros	Cons
Can fit home chores/school run/gym in between work.	Isolating, loss of social network and grapevine.
No commuting.	Outside corporate structure: bonus payments, training, promotion, awaydays etc.
Can dress down (even wear pyjamas . . .).	May not get plum assignments.
Save money on clothes, travel etc.	If you have visitors or co-workers, your home must be safe.
Efficient working between different clients.	Can you shut the door at night?
Low overheads.	Have to discipline yourself to work.
	If clients or customers visit, do you want people in your house?
	No techie immediately on hand to fix IT glitches.

❛ *Not being taken seriously is a big disadvantage of working from home. Friends dropping by when they see your car in the drive, family expecting you to just drop everything for them, working long hours often late into the night because the office is there.* ❜

Wendy Howard, Spirit of Venus

❛ *I usually work from home but also have a Gold Card with Regus which enables me to use their business lounges anywhere in the world. I use the Southampton airport Parkway office and the Euston Road one in London. They are great places to work and provide a professional environment to conduct consultations with clients.* ❜

Samantha Russell, Sardine Web Design

Pros and cons: Working on site

Pros	Cons
More sociable.	Still may not be part of the 'team'.
Access to grapevine – greater inclusion in corporate activity.	May feel like being employed.
No intrusion into your home.	May be given dogsbody work.
No home distractions.	Might be moved around office or region so no permanent base.
No responsibility for premises, safety etc.	Have to commute.
Support of corporate structure IT, HR etc.	You'll probably need to get your head down and work harder than staff, who have fewer time constraints.

Pros and cons: Acquiring your own office

Pros	Cons
Could create a better work discipline for you.	An immediate overhead that affects the bottom line.
You may want the sense of 'going to work' even if it's just down the road.	There isn't a huge range of small business premises, so you might not find anything to suit.

Keeps work out of the house, offers storage.

Can get complex, with leases, insurance, health and safety. A unit in a business centre is simpler.

An office share with others in your field of work can be collegiate and supportive. You may be able to share work.

If you share and you fall out with colleagues, what happens? If you have to leave, your business is homeless.

Helps you leave problems 'at work'.

Some issues to consider when working from home

■ You can allocate a portion of 'rent' and electricity as costs against your business (thus bringing down your tax bill). Discuss this with your accountant if you have one.

■ If your business takes over a specific part of your home, with name plates on the door, you might need to register for business rates. Check this with your local authority.

■ If clients or customers visit your home, you should have public liability insurance. See 'Insurance' in Appendix.

■ Get your security sorted out: home intrusion; computer hacking, theft or breakdown.

■ Have reliable computer backup. Work out alternatives if other equipment fails. Don't leave your computer in a car.

■ If you hold information, you may need to be registered with the Data Protection Agency. See Appendix.

■ If you have substantial car mileage for business, insure your car correctly. If you don't declare business usage and it's obvious, in a claim, that you were driving on business, you may have your claim denied.

■ Do you want people to know your home address? Does it look good? If not, you can get a postal box address, so you have to go and collect your mail.

CHAPTER NINE

IS THERE A SABOTEUR AT WORK?

We've talked about procrastination earlier when we considered setting up, but you may have to stay on your case after you get going. Coaches and psychologists love the idea of the saboteur: no, not a shady figure breaking in at night – YOU! Confidence can waiver and fear can crop up at any time, especially if things don't go to plan. The saboteur is the little voice on your shoulder saying,

'You knew this wouldn't work, I don't know why you started.'
'You? A consultant? Don't make me laugh!'
'What about your family? Don't they come first?'

What or who helped you overcome your blocks to get started? Can you rekindle that help now? Many people starting in business find their adviser or coach invaluable and if you are a waiverer, it could be worth investing in someone to help you. A partner or family member could be equally helpful, but sometimes it needs someone who is unbiased and who listens to you. Keep sight of your original goals and motivations.

Recognise your potential weaknesses

I'll get started after lunch...
Self discipline is linked to motivation, but it can be devious. We've talked in Chapter 3 about procrastination and Chapter 5 about personality traits. Take action: a course, a self-help book, a coach.

I know it's here somewhere...
Are you organised? If you aren't, you need some basic training (time management, systems) because you won't survive working for yourself. Whether online or on paper, there is a lot of information to store: emails, Word and other documents, hard copy outputs, billing, miscellaneous paperwork.

Work out your own filing system; perhaps keep a record of your file names and what they contain, where things are stored. Set up email files per subject or client. Get some funky desk equipment that holds current paperwork accessibly and stores archived work. If you are used to keeping track of things in your head, you may find it's not possible when you have several clients, numerous contacts and different projects going on.

There's plenty of time...

You have your deadlines and can prioritise your tasks. You have estimated how long a job will take you . . . so, if that report is due at midday on Wednesday . . . and it will take two days, how does your logic go? 'I'll start Monday . . . I know! I could go to the gym first thing . . . I'll start at 11am . . . sorted!' Then you find that two of the three people you have to interview for the report are away on holiday. Crash!

What's going on here? Is this something about not taking yourself seriously? Or do you like the thrill of *just* beating the deadline? Is that how you get your kicks? Well, really! Put deadlines in your diary, with big pink stickies and then work to a deadline a few days or a week before that.

Be honest with yourself

If any of the following quotes were reasons for becoming self employed then there's a good chance you won't have the required self discipline:

- 'Just to see if it works'
- 'Because I can't stand having a boss'
- 'I don't have to get up early'
- 'I'm obsessed with this, it's all I want to do'

Getting work in, planning workflow, delivering on time, billing and ensuring cash flow. It can't be done without being serious and rigorous about it.

Mind you, those reasons seem to describe most of the internet billionaires who irritatingly pop up every few weeks . . . so maybe you've got a good chance after all.

CHAPTER TEN

HEY! THAT WASN'T MEANT TO HAPPEN

Even if you truly, *truly* do not sabotage yourself, a business can waiver for any number of other reasons. It can be a shock after the effort and enthusiasm of launching to find something goes wrong. Confidence can get shaky if despondency sets in.

> ❝ I had to change my original ideas as the IT training market doesn't really exist in this climate; so I've moved into other IT support areas like troubleshooting, blogging, CRM systems, support, website review and purchasing. I have work/family conflict all the time which makes me now wonder if self employment is really for me. For the last six months I feel like I've been working from early in the morning to late at night, most weekends and no breaks. I am now at breaking point, really, as all of this work has not brought in very much money and I'm not sure if it's worth it. So I am now looking to return to IT contracting for a while, if only to pay the mortgage. ❞
>
> Sally MacMillan, Ask Sally

What has changed?

Not getting the revenue
Do you know why and can you do anything about it? If you didn't do any planning, you need to start analysing what's going wrong. Analysis and action are needed quickly.

Upsets and changes in your personal life
If you feel you can't juggle things to keep the business going, this is the time to call on others for help and support.

> ❝ Having a child has changed things for me. I now work part-time but find the constant juggling a bit difficult. I am treading water at the moment, while I rethink where I want to take the business. ❞
>
> Janice Taylor, Blue Sky Career Consulting

Physical disruption

Insurance is essential against things like fire and theft, but even so your bounce back is really needed. Even simple risk assessment and planning can help prepare for times when something goes wrong. Knowing what to do will limit the damage. It's like driving on your own in the middle of the night, in the middle of nowhere, and your car breaks down. Have you got your fully charged mobile? Do you have your breakdown number saved in it? Do you know where you are in order to give your location? Do you have a blanket and supply of chocolate?? That's how you need to be with your business.

It will also help you get back emotionally.

Learn a lesson about suppliers

CASE STUDY

Spirit of Venus, established and run by Wendy Howard
www.spiritofvenus.co.uk
Business: Leadership training programmes for small businesses
and entrepreneurs. Also a four-day leadership programme for
schools and life coaching workshops.

*This isn't Wendy's first business and it's down to her resilience that she now
has a thriving venture. In 2003, she went into image consultancy, a field she
had trained in. She admits that, because she wanted to get away from her
job so much, she rushed into that too quickly, without thinking things
through and doing sufficient research. She takes up the story:*

'I'd always been interested in fashion and image and I thought that
image consultancy would be nice and less stressful and that I could use
my people skills. If I'd researched this properly, I'd have discovered that
the market is saturated and I needed to create my own niche. So, I
looked into diversifying and added "made to measure" suits for men and
women to my service. I was approached by a company who said they
were all set up for me to place orders and they posted me a few samples
of fabrics and also a CD of different suits available. It all looked genuine
and I met up with one of the directors.

The meeting was in a hotel and he had company information on his
laptop. He said their head office was in the USA and that they'd bought
a 'licence' to offer these suits in the UK, having just bought over a

company from Ireland who had offered the suits there. He showed me a website and a company address, pictures etc. It all looked legitimate.

I was only given a really quick run-through on measuring and was then pestered to make orders. I should have been suspicious as the 'support' wasn't there but I really wanted this to work.

I started to place a few ads and leaflets and took a number of orders. I wasn't happy with the price breakdowns as I couldn't work out how I was going to really make a reasonable profit without taking large orders. It was very risky. But I decided to place some orders and to see how the supply chain worked. The first half dozen orders were fine; I delivered those and made a reasonable amount of profit. Customers thought the suits were great. So, I placed some more orders and the company, as always, demanded I paid them in full up front, which I did.

However, now the goods didn't arrive. The company complained to me (yes, *me*) that the orders were too small and this caused problems with shipping as things had to be in a mixed batch. They suggested I place larger orders to overcome this. I refused and demanded they either refund my money or deliver my order. The supply chain was their problem.

Then I found my calls were not answered, items didn't arrive; my customers were very angry with me and started chasing me. It was horrible. I'd paid the company a few thousand pounds, although thank goodness not the huge amount they had demanded. I traced the man's home address and went round there, and I got accused of harassing *him*!

Then to make it worse, two companies contacted me as the company had used my name and company name to take money and orders which they'd never delivered. I was absolutely horrified and went to the police. I also went to the companies to explain how I was being used and was having the liability passed on to me.'

What happened next?
'The Fraud Squad were involved after this. Companies House said they couldn't help as the company wasn't registered. They'd used a false number for VAT, as they'd never intended paying any.

Luckily I had sufficient evidence to prove I was the innocent and very hurt party and the police pushed for this all to go to court. However, the crooks got away as it was decided they'd made a bad business decision and had to fold the company.

I paid back every one of those orders that I'd personally taken, out of my personal money and that sank me into a huge deficit on my business. My credibility was rock bottom and I felt I was the most useless and gullible person ever. How could I have been so *stupid*?'

What has she learnt from this experience?
'Looking back, there were so many things I missed or just didn't check. I should have used my gut feelings and followed up the company registrations. There were warning bells I should have heard: no premises, no business cards, everything on a laptop (easy to run away with). These things are all cause for suspicion, which should have been checked.

I found out it is common for crooks to register a US based business address as a loophole. And the company they'd bought in Ireland was their "last suit scam" that they'd just closed down. But, as far as the law goes, they've just gone under. There is next-to-no support if you suffer fraud.

Check registration at Companies House, references and testimonials, and work with companies with a trackable track record. Never pay up front for an order. Negotiate terms and conditions. Have set agreements in place and adhere to them.'

How did she recover?
'I ended up going back to a job for two years to recover and then came back and re-started my business doing something I was much better at and much happier doing.'

General tips for security
- be pleasant but sceptical
- take money up front if you can
- check identities before letting workmen enter your premises
- check credentials and references thoroughly
- be wary of bogus emails or callers.

CHAPTER ELEVEN

HOW WILL YOU MARKET YOURSELF?

Marketing is the lifeblood of your business, so this will be the longest chapter of this part.

You may have your little red book of contacts and can trust the phone to ring with your next piece of work, or you may have a good recruitment agent who always has the next job for you. If you are so confident of never needing to lift a finger, lucky you! But you could challenge yourself by asking, 'Could I get more stimulating or better paid work elsewhere?'

For the rest of us, marketing and selling is vital to get work in and produce a profitable business. It is likely to be a mix of hustling our contacts, networking and cold calling. As your business and your reputation, grows, so your marketing will get more elaborate, but to begin with, keep it simple (stupid). Whoever coined that phrase?

Do your planning

The majority of micro businesses will grab a few ideas and launch:

Let's do the website . . . Get some cards printed . . . Go to that drinks evening/conference/exhibition . . . Start tweeting . . . er, that's it.

And these might be really good ideas, but how can you be sure? Some of that activity will cost money which might not be well spent.

> ❛ I wish I hadn't wasted money on advertising and all those mundane charity calendars etc, (emotional decisions). By all means "support" one if your cash flow allows, but there are much easier and less expensive ways of getting your message out there. ❜
>
> Wendy Howard, Director, Spirit of Venus

TRY THIS

A good marketing plan will stand you in good stead. Here's the process:

Task	Purpose
Describe your service	This is more than, 'I am a copy writer'. Give an accurate statement of what you do and how you deliver it – on site, by the hour, by project etc. It's also what makes you stand out in your field. This is termed your 'unique selling proposition' (USP). You may need to research the competition, but this becomes the core of your sales message.
Describe your client base	Which individuals, by job title, are your targets? Who are they – individual professionals, small businesses, large businesses, public sector? What sector/industry are they in? Are they busy professionals (who might not understand your skill), procurement specialists (looking for discount, best value etc.) or people just like you (so they know exactly what you do)?
How do they purchase?	Do you know if and when they might need your service? Is there a strict tendering process? Is it a cosy world of who you know? Will they search the internet? Are they influenced by marketing messages? Are there referrers involved? Is it a price-sensitive market? Will they want you to start the next day or plan months in advance?

This will give you a good base for the next stage:

What 'profile' do you need?	A website? Expert articles placed in the press? Good marketing literature? Creative logo or serious note head? Speaking platforms?
How do you get face to face?	What are the expert forums and social occasions? Are you part of the industry? Can you phone and suggest a coffee, or 'credentials' presentation? Can you get on the tendering list?
What is your key message?	If you've worked out your USP and you know what the client really needs, build around this. For instance, 'I have 10 years' experience of IT systems in the medical sector.' (*Specialist expertise*)

	'In my previous job I negotiated settlements in three complex unfair dismissal tribunals.' (*Tough negotiator*) 'My website designs have won two awards in the past year.' (*Creative flair*)
Marketing materials	Creative identity. Stationery. Website, blogging, tweeting. Literature or brochure.
Promotional activity – according to what suits	Speaking platforms. Article writing. Surveys. Networking. Awards. Exhibition space. Advertising. Offers, e.g., two-hour training 'demo'. What is the competition doing?
Budget	Have you set a budget? Cost everything you want to do from the above. Can you afford it? What is necessary as opposed to nice to do? Then cut according to budget or what you think you should spend. Don't do it all at once; prioritise and then add other things as you earn.

And then once you get going:

Evaluate	You *must* build in measurement systems where you can see what works. Web visits and responses; ask where enquirers heard of you; response advertising. Get and follow up leads from all face-to-face activity and analyse work gained. Build all these results into your plan and adjust activity.

From this you will have:
- ► What you are selling
- ► Who your target is
- ► What your key message is
- ► How to get noticed
- ► How to get a meeting
- ► How to adjust your activity
- ► Accuracy of budget

What skills will I need?

You are selling yourself – your time and expertise – and you are probably selling to a knowledgeable or professional audience. Communication and interpersonal skills are vital. So you'll need:

Skill required	**Encounter**
Good interview technique (both ways)	A basic enquiry and meeting
Confidence to approach people, introduce yourself and engage in conversation	Networking and other social events
Selling skills	Exhibitions, presentations, telephone calls, credentials pitches, sales meetings, pitches and tenders
Personable demeanour and positive outlook	'Nice people to do business with'

❝ I did research into which product to use for the online classroom and took the plunge to buy it. On 1 September 2008, I went to the local networking breakfast. This took a bit of courage but from here I was introduced to the whole concept of networking which has proved to be invaluable in terms of support, services and clients. ❞

Mary Thomas, Concise Training

If any of this looks daunting, get advice – some mentioned in this book! There are marketing consultants available. If you lack any of the skills above, seek training. With the demise of Business Link, it is worth budgeting for training.

A three-stage plan for the freelancer

Your marketing plan might be timed in the following way:

Stage I (Months 1–2: pre-launch)
- Get your proposition clear and on paper.
- Produce your stationery and website if necessary.
- Research your targets (potential clients).
- Make some phone calls or go to a networking group. Get a couple of credentials meetings if possible (and use these for research as well).
- Write an article or get booked on a conference platform.

❝ Having had encouragement from my husband, family and a couple of respected business contacts, I went ahead with emailing business contacts about my experience and setting up the business. I was extraordinarily fortunate to have my first client before I even had my business name *organised. A company that was in a networking group I have attended for four years needed a marketing plan, and help to deliver it, for the launch of three new, innovative products.* '

Emma Pearce, Pearce Marketing Consultants

Stage II (Months 3–6: launch and post-launch)

- Inform all your contacts of your launch – tra laaaa!
- Send mailer or email to your targets.
- Build up your promotional activity as required. Only spend what is planned and budgeted.
- Get listed in directories as required.
- Attend networking group/s as guest and join most worthwhile.
- Develop your presentation/pitch.
- Get training as required.
- More phone calls, more meetings/credentials presentations. Can you get on a pitch list?

Stage III (Months 6–12: developing)

- Develop promotional activity, building up budget if available.
- Continue credentials presentations, pitches/tenders.
- Continue networking and socialising (it's hard, but someone's got to do it).
- Blog, tweet, develop online presence according to need.
- Learn from all meetings and from work you get.
- Enter that superb project you've done for an award!

This is a kitchen sink list and you won't need to do all of this. Some people manage without stationery; others without websites and plenty still haven't got the hang of blogging and tweeting. You'll find viewpoints in this book for and against networking. So it's very much up to your market and your personal style. Think about what you feel is essential, what the market tends to expect and what suits you.

Sell, sell, sell

Unless you are *extremely* lucky with word-of-mouth referrals, the one thing you will need to do is SELL! Cold calling isn't on many people's list of favourite activities, hence the networking and socialising so that you can end the conversation with, 'Perhaps we could have a coffee sometime. Could I call you?' But however you do it, you have to make the initial approach to a complete stranger.

First approach

Cold calling nowadays is by a phone call, email or letter. In a business or professional environment, texting or sending a social networking invitation would overstep the boundaries. (LinkedIn might be acceptable.)

It isn't easy, as the dreaded voicemail is so often left on. And, of course, if you don't know who your target is, you have to research names and titles. There's no magic answer as to which channel works best, but let's look at the pros and cons.

Communication approach	Pros	Cons
Telephone	The most effective way to persuade.	People get irritated by sales calls; voicemail often on. Companies often block cold callers, especially if you ask for them by job title.
Email	Cheap. Instant. Can be effective if eye catching.	Could go into spam box. Could be deleted without being read. Make sure your contact is legal (see page 111).
Post	Chance to create visual impact and explain your service.	Could be binned before it gets to intended recipient. More expensive, especially if with printed literature.

If you have done any sales like this, you'll know it's a thankless task. You could make 20 calls which go to voicemail and then be so surprised to get through to one you forget your opening line. You really only have one chance at a call or meeting, so be on the ball all the time.

Before you make any contact think, 'What do I want to achieve?' This could be:

- Finding out if they use your service.
- Agreeing to a casual, introductory meeting.
- A presentation, perhaps to get on a list of suppliers.
- A chance to pitch, if they have a project coming up.
- Arranging to meet at a conference or networking.

Start by introducing yourself, asking some questions about how they fill the need (that you offer), how happy they are with the existing service and then hit them with how you could do it better. Try to avoid questions they can answer with a 'Yes' or 'No' (closed). For instance:

> Have you thought about offering fire-eating classes to your staff? *(Yes)*
> Do you offer these classes, then? *(Yes)*
> Do you need anyone else – I'd light up the place? *(No, thank you)*

Instead:

> What would be a fun way for your staff to stay motivated at work? *(Well, we run fire-eating classes)*
> Oh, you already do fire-eating classes? Tell me how they are going? *(Oh, they're really hot)*
> Ah, you keep having to call ambulances? Well, let me tell you about my health and safety record *(Ok, then)*
> Better still, why don't I come in and give you a demonstration? Next Thursday? *(Ok, see you then)*

Or perhaps you have some research findings or information you could tell them about (not necessarily on pyrotechnics). It may be that they have a seasonal pattern of commissioning work. You are looking for a little chink of light you can begin to work on. If they are mildly responsive, see if you can get the meeting (suggesting a cup of coffee sounds quite informal and not too long). A combination of two forms of contact could be more productive; say, sending a letter (or email) and following up by phone.

Keep in mind: you're brilliant at what you do!

The meeting

If you get a meeting, plan your informal presentation. You could take a small laptop if you want to get information and data across, or a small presentation pack.

Tips
- Don't make it unwieldy or too dependent on technology. Fantastic as Powerpoint is, it's pretty overused these days, so don't sit and read out bullet points.
- It's more informal if you can remain seated, sit next to, or at an angle of 45 degrees from the other person.

■ Sitting opposite is somewhat confrontational and it's difficult to share information.

■ Avoid too much light or the sun in your eyes; sitting too near the radiator and so on.

■ If you meet in a coffee shop (very trendy), make sure it's not too busy and that you can get privacy.

What do you want to get out of the meeting?

■ Find out how they operate, what potential there is for you.

■ A mutual exchange of information and leave your card.

■ The first step to a friendly business relationship.

■ To get on a list of preferred suppliers, or pitch list.

■ To secure a 'taster' session (e.g., demo or training session).

■ Or even . . . a sale!

'Every hour away from base must be used efficiently. The object of selling is to get orders. Each face-to-face call must have that end in view. Perhaps not on the first visit, but each call should end with a new bit of information of use along the road. Good accounts need working on. Remember, there is always a competitor in there already, possibly cheaper, invariably satisfactory, but above all – known.'[2]

The pitch or presentation

If your market selects in this formal way and you don't have much experience of presenting it's a good idea to get a training course or a couple of books. An internet search reveals plenty of courses or ask colleagues at network events.

Some tips

■ You will have questions on the brief. Talk to the contact to find out what they want. They might be prepared to meet you beforehand.

■ Do research on the company; its market and competitors; the specifics of your field and the job they want to have done.

■ Try to find out who else is pitching. What advantage/s do you have over them?

■ Find out who you will be presenting to; know who the key decision taker is, who has a lot of influence.

■ Ask where you will be presenting, make sure the technology is compatible (or take your laptop). Tell them your requirements.

■ Arrive early and ask if you can set up to get your positioning, the presentation ready and think about how/if you can move around.

■ A nice little gesture is to take some mints or fruit sweets in a small bowl to pass round. It's memorable.

■ How long will it be? How much information do they need? What message will you leave them with? Examples of previous work, perhaps a small case study, are vital (not easy if you are just starting up).

■ Always be honest: don't claim experience you don't have or try to answer a question you really don't know the answer to.

■ Will you leave a supporting document/s behind?

■ Ask when they will make a decision.

■ Tell them how much you'd like to work with them and hope they would like to work with you.

Presenting with a team

You may well present with a team. If so, be clear what your relationship with each person is; clients are used to virtual teams nowadays but they don't like deception. Explain how you can manage the project if you're not all under one roof.

Then go and debrief over a drink!

Getting the decision

You may have to chase them for a decision and, believe it or not, some people never respond. It's disrespectful of your time, but another thing to put under that thickening skin. And above all, learn to take rejection and try not to see it as personal. You know the one about kissing a lot of frogs . . . the genuine, lovable clients are out there too! And the disappointment is balanced by the times when you are appointed.

You'll get the idea now that selling yourself can be a hard business. Your business is close to your heart and you have to be outgoing and confident, but honest about your limitations. Learn from each experience and build up a portfolio of work and recommendations as you go along (get permission from clients if you are reproducing their work or using testimonials).

What should you spend on marketing?

This will depend on:

- how much money you have to start
- your projected sales/income for the first year
- the norms of the market.

Five per cent of your projected income is a rough guide for a launch as you'll have set-up costs that aren't repeated every year (the run on cost of printing is quite low so print a good supply of stationery and cards to begin with). You probably don't need to advertise if your market is corporate, but listings in directories or freelance websites might be useful. Joining the right networking groups and attending, say, one event a month, will be between £500 and £1,000 a year. You can do a lot of your own public relations, and writing articles or speaking are free (don't pay to place an article unless you know that particular magazine works).

This marketing programme is geared towards reputation building (rather than brand building). To develop as a freelance or contractor you need to:

Get your name known, and known for what you do.	Good corporate identity (stationery/website); strapline (what you do); listings.
Meet your key targets.	Direct approach/pitches; networking.
Promote your knowledge.	Article writing; speaking platforms.
Connect.	Tweeting, blogging, social networking.

Getting together

Networking is hugely popular among business people, especially the self employed. The number of groups is growing all the time. Here's just a selection:

- Women only networking – for support and business.
- Local businesses – i.e., Chamber of Commerce.

- Pitch breakfasts – finding each other work.
- Industry/professional groups – networking and training.
- Exclusive 'category' – just one person from every field.

> ❝ *Networking is very important and particularly for my type of business, it is my main marketing/lead generation source. I am a member of the manufacturing ProfitNetGroup – that was my employer's business and the group allowed me to stay in when I left. I have also joined a women's group for the first time. I was never sure if they were right for me before but now I need to break into all areas to build a business.* ❞
>
> Emma Pearce, Pearce Marketing Consultants

> ❝ *I have found networking invaluable. I do both women only networks and mixed but I have probably found mixed networking better. I have clients, services and support on the networking circuit. I've taken the attitude that nobody is going to find me unless I get out there and market myself.* ❞
>
> Mary Thomas, Concise Training

But be selective as to what suits you and at what stage in your business:

> ❝ *It's a very important way for me to get to grips with the way that business is done. I've met some great contacts, although not as many customers as I had hoped. I think I am now actually "burnt out" by networking and the thought of having to stand up and say "Hi, my name is Sally from Ask Sally" is not an appealing thought.* ❞
>
> Sally MacMillan, Ask Sally

> ❝ *At the very beginning, I was invited to many business networking clubs; they assured me if I joined (for a huge fee) there will be masses of business coming my way. My business does not fit well into the "boys network". Chocolate is more often a personal purchase, not a business purchase.* ❞
>
> Jackie Roberts, The Chocolate Tailor

So, find your local and professional groups, go along as a guest before you join and become part of the ones that offer the right mix for your business.

And of course, networking is now online and may help your business.

> ❝ *Twitter has helped me in a number of ways: firstly I keep in contact with people that I have met face to face but don't see very often. Secondly, since I*

have been on Twitter, I have used it to build my brand and reputation. I'm hopefully seen as "an expert" in the subject area of IT. And thirdly, I offer Twitter training courses to help others talk to their customers through Twitter.

Has Twitter added to my bottom line? Yes, in that I am delivering Twitter training in both face-to-face courses and individual online courses. I think this will grow over the next year or so. It's difficult to quantify whether my tweets have directly led to business. I don't link to my website enough – my marketing is probably not as direct as it should be. This will need to change to pick up clients directly from Twitter.

Mary Thomas, Concise Training

I use LinkedIn, to keep in touch with people, to find out about people that I am going to train and I also train in using LinkedIn. I have a presence on other social media sites: viadeo, wecandobiz, startupcommunity, junction31, business women's cafe, women's business club and others. Although my profiles need updating, they still drive traffic to my website and ultimately to me. I have a few clients who found me through these social media sites and therefore we have never actually met. This is a great free way of marketing for me!

Mary Thomas, Concise Training

This section could go into much more detail. There are lots of helpful books you can borrow or buy as well as training courses available and consultants to help (including two of our contributors!).

CHAPTER TWELVE

COLLABORATION

Collaboration with colleagues can help you grow your business and provide much needed company and brain storming. Partnering, best friends and other such arrangements have become fashionable more recently, even among big business, so it is worth looking into. It might be with other practitioners doing the same work as you or people offering complementary services, that could be purchased at the same time. For instance:

■ A holistic therapy clinic with rooms for a chiropractor, an acupuncturist, a reiki healer, a reflexologist, yoga and meditation classes. The focus would be on the premises, with each business being promoted under that 'umbrella', or brand name.

■ A marketing communications service, such as corporate designer, PR consultant, web consultant and advertising planner/media buyer.

■ Three corporate writers pooling to market their services for annual reports, brochures etc., sharing out work according to specialism and availability.

Grouping together in one place can create a brand even though the participants are independent of each other.

Be part of a virtual team

Working as a virtual team, each from your own workplace, enables you to pitch for business that you wouldn't be considered for on your own. In the case of marketing, for instance, clients often want consistency across their communications and they don't want to deal with lots of individuals. However, they don't necessarily want to use a big agency and pay a premium.

TRY THIS

Weigh up the pros and cons for you

Pros	Cons
Hiring premises can be simple as you just rent a room and pay towards reception etc.	You should consider a contract to clarify your relationship as a tenant and your liability towards clients.
Marketing can be transformed by being part of a group of practitioners. You can share costs.	Don't take part in anything that makes you appear to be part of someone else's business, unless you are sure of your position.
You have company with like-minded people (when you are not head down working!)	How do you each bill clients when you are working on a project together?
You can take on bigger projects for bigger clients.	The quality, or continuity of your business is affected by others.
	If you all do the same work and business is slow, how do you share out new work?
	What if one of you is approached independently?
	Do you pool income?

Protect your business

You will no doubt find other advantages and disadvantages for your circumstances. As ever, you need to allow for the worst possible scenario: if you rent premises and market under an umbrella, what if the mortgage holder defaults on payments? If you work as a virtual team and some of the work goes wrong, where does the liability rest? What if the client doesn't pay at all? What if a client visits you, specifically, and is injured coming into the premises, and sues you? You can't always prevent such events but you can be prepared for them.

Be wary of going into formal arrangements unless you are sure of your colleagues:

❝ *I made a huge mistake of going into business with two other women, which cost me £35,000. The money was supposed to be coming through joint investing, but no one put any money in. So I have spent the last two years working hand-to-mouth, investing everything into my ideas and developing services and products.* ❯

Karen Purves, Centre for Effective Marketing

It all sounds fearful, but you have to protect yourself with a clear contract and appropriate insurance, and ensure that colleagues, landlords and so on have the right liability insurance. Be clear to clients what your relationship with your team is and have one lead business that holds the contract with the client.

❝ *I am starting to develop relationships with associates and partners. I am having a meeting with a Photoshop tutor this week regarding using my online classroom to deliver his training course. Things are developing all the time!* ❯

Mary Thomas, Concise Training

❝ *I work alone but use contractors where necessary. I'll use contract designers, developers and search engine optimisers.* ❯

Samantha Russell, Sardine Web Design

Summary checklist: The expert

- ✓ Make sure you have the right qualifications and other requirements to work in the market.
- ✓ Write down the pros and cons for you of going freelance.
- ✓ Ensure your tax status is set up correctly.
- ✓ Do your financial planning.
- ✓ Research the pay rates or fees and set yours according to experience.
- ✓ Budget for two years before you hit your target earnings.
- ✓ Brush up on your negotiation skills.
- ✓ Set up timesheets and use them.
- ✓ Ensure all work is profitable – don't over service.
- ✓ Establish good invoicing processes.
- ✓ Decide where to work.
- ✓ Address any blocks or weaknesses.
- ✓ Be prepared for problems or crises.
- ✓ Write a marketing plan.
- ✓ Consider working with others, but be cautious.

Part 3:
Setting Up a
Small Business

Introduction

In this part we'll look at setting up a small business with the focus on trading. It will often start at home; growth may well be planned and initially, organic. This is more complex than selling your time, and demands more financing up front. From internet commerce to recruitment to repairing cars to software training . . . the list goes on.

We'll look at the challenges of setting up a business: the motivation, marketing and – oh yes – financing it all. The dreaded business plan rears its head here. We'll see what challenges and opportunities are specific to women. And we'll meet women who have achieved real success, and others who are meeting challenges, as entrepreneurs.

Women run any and every kind of business, even in typically male dominated sectors. These include IT, newspapers, manufacturing and engineering, science and biotech, banking and finance. However, there are some typical fields that attract women:

- Exploiting their expertise in the service sector such as recruitment, marketing and IT (Part Two).

- The beauty and hairdressing business; plus many areas of health and complementary therapies (see Case Study Yana Cosmetics, below).

- The growing field of homeworking (Chapter 24); including 'mumpreneur' internet businesses selling anything and everything to do with babies (Chapter 25).

- Another growth area is direct selling. From 'Avon Calling' to a whole industry of products sold face-to-face, mostly by women (Chapter 27).

CHAPTER THIRTEEN

MOTIVATION, AMBITION, OPPORTUNITY

Why do you want to start a business?

A YouGov survey[3] commissioned for the Government Equalities Office in May 2008 found that the majority of women (70%) become self employed in order to have flexibility in their family life. Other motivators to starting a business were:

- to be their own boss (65%)
- to be able to work from home (61%)
- to get more job satisfaction (53%)
- to achieve a better work/life balance (52%).

There are personal gains too:

- more than three quarters (78%) gained greater independence from setting up their own business
- two thirds (66%) increased confidence
- 60% said it gave them greater self-worth.

What else do you need?

Everyone needs motivation in order to slog away to build a business, but often a little opportunity helps too. The businesses we are looking at here are start-ups, rather than pre-existing, inherited or purchased businesses. That's not to detract from the achievement of women who have developed a family business, but here we are looking at original ideas.

Having a helping hand does not guarantee success. However, some people are in better starting situations than others. For instance:

Coming into money

A windfall can come from inheritance, redundancy or even winning the lottery. The circumstances might not always be happy ones, but having some finance behind you is a huge confidence booster. Not only do you have start-up capital, you also have money to keep you going before you are profitable enough to start taking an income. And even if it doesn't cover all you need, it's an encouragement to other lenders or investors.

> ❮ At the end of July 2007, the IT Department at my work was outsourced and I was made redundant. The process dragged on for about a year and a half leaving me with low confidence levels, a lack of faith in large corporate organisations and a desire to keep my freedom.
>
> With the redundancy package acting as a cushion, I felt I had more options and started to think about setting up my own web design business. I'd been teaching myself web design for two years prior to leaving and had built several successful websites for friends and family that not only looked good but generated business too. If I got another job, I would have to commit to that for at least two years, again putting off my dream of having my own business. So, really, it was now or never. Why not give it six months and see where I had got to by then?
>
> It's one of the best decisions I ever made. Now, over two years later, I feel like a different person and someone who is totally in control of her life. ❯
>
> Samantha Russell, Sardine Web Design

Another breadwinner in the house

Women can't claim many advantages in the workplace or business arena, especially if they have children. But if you have a partner who continues to bring in a decent salary and benefits, the worry is undoubtedly reduced. We'll come to financing and risking the roof over your head in Chapter 18.

Setting up with friend/colleague

Sometimes an idea evolves with a colleague and sometimes that collaboration produces a successful business (see Case Study on SK Chase, Chapter 14). There is more to work out when you go into business with someone else, and any income will be split into two. But ideas can often develop better with two, possibly complementary, minds. Two people can generate confidence where maybe on their own they might not move forward. And of course, there are two people to do the work.

Having an entrepreneurial background

Parents, partners or friends who are in business are definitely a spur for many people. Growing up with the daily life of a business breeds familiarity and confidence, plus you know about the challenges. It doesn't necessarily mean those people are the best to advise you, but they are very often an inspiration and help.

' *My aunt was an entrepreneur and had previously had many businesses; and if she wasn't afraid to lose then neither was I.* '

Yana Johnson MBE, Yana Cosmetics

Losing your job

It's now familiar: every recession throws up new businesses. While job loss, closure and the disappearance of entire industries are sad events, many people find it the impetus to set up on their own. They find personal resources they weren't aware of when they were employed; and for many it's a new (if demanding) lease of life. A few of our case studies started their business when their job either ended or became untenable.

Natural break/not going back

Some job breaks (such as maternity leave or sabbatical) are for positive reasons. Others might be for illness, family-caring demands or even disciplinary reasons. Such occasions can produce reflection and soul searching about what you want from life and whether employment is right for you any longer. This can provide the impetus and even the creative spark needed to start a venture, especially if backed up by some finance. This is the subject of Part Four.

How ambitious are you?

Ambition is one of those words many women shy away from. When you watch a whodunit, you know that any woman portrayed as ambitious is either going to get the chop or be the murderer. Where, one wonders, are the nasty, ambitious men, or the 'career boys'?

Compared with men, few women start out with a plan to rival Marks and Spencer within 10 years. But ambition is different for everyone: for one person it could be building a scalable business with a multi-million pound turnover; for others it might be getting out of unemployment and supporting themselves.

TRY THIS
It is a question worth asking yourself: How do I feel about being ambitious? How ambitious will I need to be to make a living from this?

What is the business potential?

Potential can, of course, be seen very broadly. It could mean the potential to change lives, or make a particular task easier, or provide employment for a community. Here, however, we'll consider potential in terms of demand and thus the sales growth plans you could create.

An example of two different businesses

Compare a children's face painting venture, travelling within a 20 mile radius of your home, with a City-based recruitment business with the potential to go global. How do you forecast or estimate demand? You could do this top down or bottom up.

For the face painting venture, you may simply say, 'I am going to aim for 30 customers a week from three events.' That would be bottom up, based on what you think you can supply. And you might simply set up and work towards achieving that. There's not much to lose except, say, £100 and some strange looking children at first.

The recruitment business would (sensibly) require top down forecasting: research into the existing market, economic and employment forecasts, the volume of jobs handled, the gaps in the market and what potential clients want from any new supplier. From that research you could begin to put numbers on the jobs you might get and fill (forecasting). Growth plans are developed as your reputation grows.

How does risk make you feel?

Many of the self-employed women featured in this book view risk as losing money. 'As long as I didn't lose money I was prepared to give it a try,' was a common response. Money is likely to be a central part of our view of risk. So how do you view the following scenarios?

Investment decisions

'I spent £500 on a new logo and stationery and I was earning £1,500 a month straight away. Result!'

Sounds good, but what if an investment of £5,000, that enabled you to advertise, brought in £25,000 in the first year?

'I have £25,000 to invest in my business. My adviser thinks I should raise £60,000 in total to do it properly and get through the first year.'

So where are you going to get the extra funding from? How do you feel about a loan? Might you consider giving away some equity?

'My accountant says I should double my price and build my client base among those who can afford to pay more. But I don't feel that's right as many people on low income need my service. And what if I lose too many customers?'

It's a dilemma, especially if you have built in a social or ethical stance to your business. Offering an affordable (but efficient) service can be feasible, as can a premium service. If both ways stack up profitably it will come down to a choice based on your values.

Women start up in business with lower financing than men (see Raising Finance, Chapter 18); this is an indication of ambition and attitude to risk. It inevitably limits the growth potential of the business, at least to begin with.

Financially, your planning will be done on a range of projections from best to worst, and your adviser would plump for the one in the lower middle as being the most realistic. So you have to answer the questions, 'What happens if I only do ok; or badly?', 'Can I afford to lose this money?', 'Can I continue if I make a loss to begin with?' Doing some financial projections and preparing yourself for losses (money-wise and emotionally) will make for a better survival strategy.

On the whole, women are more risk averse than men. Also, women judge their success on a broader range of outcomes so in reality, risk to a female entrepreneur doesn't mean just money. It conjures up different fears and concerns, even if they can't be quantified:

What else is connected to risk?
- Loss of reputation/status.
- Fear of failure.
- Fear of success.
- Losing the house.
- Neglecting the family.
- Neglecting the partner/husband.
- Divorce.
- Producing a bad product.
- Letting staff down.
- Letting the community down.

TRY THIS

In your planning/reflecting stage it is useful to think about what might be risky to you, how realistic that concern is and what you can do to reduce (mitigate) it.

❝ My attitude to risk is that I am quite risk averse but I do like to challenge myself. I am ambitious and that drive helped me overcome my risk aversion. I didn't do a risk analysis before setting up; I just gave myself six months to see where I got to. At the end of the first six months, I quickly realised this wasn't nearly enough time and gave myself another six months. ❞

Samantha Russell, Sardine Web Design

According to research[3] fear of failure is a significant concern for 27% of women in business and a minor concern for 44%. If it makes you feel more confident, actual failure rates are 'on a par for both male and female entrepreneurs'.

Female-led businesses in summary

On the whole, women start and run smaller businesses than men do and businesses that have unfulfilled potential because they:

- have different goals from men
- are less ambitious
- are more risk averse
- perceive discrimination over financing[4]
- do not realise the potential of their business
- under-capitalise (don't raise enough money)[5]
- have time limitations
- are concerned about their family quality of life
- will not risk their relationship.

Before you shout, 'That's not me!', not *all* women tick *all* the above boxes – some tick none! And of course *some* men tick *some* of the above boxes as well (hurrah for family life!). But these are factors that need to be studied when government and banks are developing policy in this area (i.e., childcare, access to financing). They are also challenges you need to consider right at the beginning when you have that spark of inspiration.

Have faith in yourself and others

CASE STUDY

Yana Cosmetics, established and run by Yana Johnson MBE
www.yanacosmetics.com
Business: Yana Cosmetics is the only premium ethnic cosmetic brand in the UK wholly owned by a black woman. Yana Cosmetics provides

makeup and skincare and a men's skincare line available online.

Yana Johnson is a successful business woman and a 'make-up mogul'. After graduating from the University of Greenwich she went on to open concessions in what she calls a 'humble' department store and hairdressing salon in Brixton, London. She recognised the difficulty ethnic and black people had in finding the right cosmetics so she developed her brand Yana Cosmetics in 2001. Yana was awarded an MBE for her services to cosmetics, pioneering her makeup and skincare line for ethnic and black people in the UK. Her approach is both businesslike and spiritual.

'My decision to start was basically to solve a problem that I had experienced first-hand. This was a lack of representation, understanding and translation of makeup products to the ethnic market. The first Yana Cosmetics store opened with a strong team of professionals and high demand from day one. Coming from a media background, I was aware of what was necessary to market and grow my brand on a very professional level, with the emphasis on excellence. I worked hard to train a team of makeup artists and establish immaculate customer service. The business has been built on its integrity.

I feel that empowering people and making them look and feel good is a spiritual thing because it's a positive way of extending love. Caring about the needs of a market is also ethical. I take corporate and social responsibility seriously.'

How did she get started and what support did she get?
'I had a lot of sound advice from professional people and I worked hard at networking and observing people for consistency. I was educated on how to conduct my business and believe that if you have a gut feeling, then follow it. My friends with businesses were able to point out pitfalls that I could avoid. I felt that I was fast tracked and guided the whole time. If you are keen to observe practices and repeat the successful ones, you develop a business methodology that will not fail.'

What has her background brought to the venture?
'The inspiration to achieve and operate outside of fear has been instilled in me from a very young age by my father. I am a very creative individual and he always encouraged me. Yana Cosmetics was an idea that I knew I would enjoy and that had great potential.

I had no fears, which may not always be a good thing. However, I have a great problem-solving attitude which means that I was ready to try everything. I also aligned myself with positive people who encouraged me when they saw potential and corrected me with problem-solving advice when I was in need of advice.

My aunt, who was an entrepreneur, invested £1,000 and told me to go get my dream. She always believed in me and I never looked back. Having one person who believes in you is great because you have encouragement (although *too many* people saying 'Yes' can blind you into thinking it's all good). My father and uncles were both self employed, so seeing that from an early age gave me a natural feel for business.'

What challenges has she faced?
'Life is a balancing act and as a single working professional mother, challenges come in all shapes and sizes. From cash flow, to manpower, to creative deadlines; all scream for number one position for attention. You have to master the art of prioritising and then rest.'

What are her values, for family and business?
'What God has given me is special; it is a legacy and an inheritance for my daughter (who also has her own brand, RedYella). She will not go through life ever thinking that she cannot do something. I have released that blessing to her and hopefully many others who know the Yana story. Again, balance your day right: eat every meal together at the table, bringing traditional family values. No matter what the schedule, this keeps everyone bonded and in tune. My Christian faith is also the rock that holds everything in my life together.'

How is the business developing?
'I have expanded the brand by launching the Yana Make-up Representative Programme (YMR). This is a network of women, offering them empowerment through reselling Yana make up.'

> ❝ *Women in ethnic minority communities are more likely to be entrepreneurial than their white counterparts for all categories except "other Asian". Black African women are more likely to be entrepreneurial than men (18.9% of women compared to 15.7% of men) and are nearly four-and-a-half times more likely than their white counterparts to be entrepreneurially active. The equivalent figure for white respondents was 3.6%.* ❞
>
> Stairways to Growth 2010[6]

CHAPTER FOURTEEN

WHAT'S YOUR IDEA?

Where do ideas come from?

Unlike big business, where millions are spent on idea generation, most small businesses are founded on inspiration or gut feeling. And often the product or service can be brought to life on a scale that tests the market and is then improved. Initial business expansion only happens when the product sells, so growth is organic and gradual.

Ideas come from anywhere.

- It's a passion.
- It's my hobby.
- I've got 20 years' experience of this.
- I thought it up in the bath.
- I dreamt about it.
- I came across it while travelling.
- I saw it and thought, 'I could do that so much better.'
- My employer just didn't see the potential.
- I couldn't find anything that did the job properly.
- I saw someone else doing it.
- Here's a supply, now surely there's a demand?
- Adults loved it, but there was nothing for kids.
- I went to a creative ideas workshop.
- I brainstormed with some friends in the winebar.

And the list could go on.

Ok, what *do* I want to do?

> ❛ As I love internet shopping and am interested in design generally, the idea of starting a design site for kids came naturally out of that. Wanting to showcase eco products came to me as something that would fit in very well with the greener lifestyle I was trying to lead and wanted for my children.❜
>
> Tabitha Harman, Mimimyne

❝ I have hankered for about 5 years now to do my own thing. However, until a couple of years ago I wasn't sure what my own thing was! I deliberated with a number of ideas from chocolate making to wedding planning and it dawned upon me that maybe, to begin with, I should stick to what I know, and that is accountancy! ❞

Emma Lodge, Balance Accounting Solutions

If you have a general idea of what market you would like to work in (your hobby, expertise), go to the places where you can get ideas and see what others are doing. It could be a Saturday market, the internet, an exhibition. Where are the gaps? What could be improved upon? Copied on a smaller scale (without copyright infringement)? Who is looking for distributors/franchisees? Talk to potential customers/friends.

Many of the women's networking sites now have ideas for businesses and they have ads for distributors and franchisees; so if you need more ideas, surf around (see Appendix).

Making it happen

Assuming you have researched the potential, carried out a small test run on friends/volunteers, set your ambition on moderate to high and got your risk profile under control, what's next?

TRY THIS
Action checklist to bring your idea to life

Production	Am I manufacturing, assembling or buying?
	How is it made?
	At what cost?
	Do I have the facilities at home or do I need premises?
	Do I need to employ people?
	Do I need training or qualifications?
	Is this feasible for me?
	Do I need to patent or protect my intellectual property?
Demand	Have I researched the market potential?
	Is the proposition clear?
	What should the price be?
	Will the market grow or change?

Marketing	How will I reach the market?
	Is this an internet business?
	Do I sell face to face?
	How much investment will this require?
	What should be in my marketing plan?
	Am I suited to this?
Lifestyle	Do I like this product/business?
	Do I have the enthusiasm/commitment for it?
	Does this business fit with my lifestyle/family commitments?
	Do I have the right personality/credibility for this business?
Official aspects	Do I require a licence to do this?
	How complex are the regulations in this business?
	Can my idea be copied or stolen easily?
	What threats could damage supply?
	What insurance will I need?

Sometimes the list of questions, and their answers, can halt the progress of your idea. But it's better that you ask them now than find out later. And if they survive this test, or lead you to more research and refining your idea, then you gain.

Test and refine your idea

When you first test or trial your idea (assuming you can) think carefully about what you are looking for. Poor responses don't necessarily mean thumbs down; ask the person for more information. Answers might refine your idea. Can you choose a real guinea pig who can answer a questionnaire afterwards and give you really good feedback? If you have a physical product, can you produce a prototype that is given a good hammering (unless its porcelain dolls, of course!).

Test things as much as you can. And if you can't test, or you just want to get on with things, make sure you get feedback from the very first clients or customers. There are very few products or services on the market that have not been improved upon.

Exploit the right idea at the right time

CASE STUDY

SK Chase, established and run by Kaye Taylor and Stephanie Wilson

www.skchase.com

Business: provides an online gift voucher application and fulfilment service to luxury hotels throughout the UK

S K Chase is the story of an idea the timing of which was perfect. Kaye and Stephanie (Steph) worked for The Town House Collection, a group of four hotels in Scotland. Both are married and, at the time of setting up, with no children. They started trading in June 2004, operating from Kaye's flat in Edinburgh. Kaye left her job six months later and Steph followed in March 2005. Kaye takes up the story in 2003:

'I had wanted to have my own business for a number of years and I had a real desire to not have a boss! I wanted the freedom of being the decision maker and being able to implement my ideas quickly and easily. I was keen to set up a business that would be scalable and based on technology, because I've always loved making things easier and better with the use of technology.

As marketing manager at The Town House Collection, I was responsible for the portfolio of websites and increasing the amount of relevant traffic to the sites, thus increasing the look-to-buy ratio (the number of people choosing to book online, rather than by phone).

During this time I realised it would be great if we could also sell a range of gift experiences online, where site visitors could browse a catalogue, select their desired experience and pay online. I assumed that other luxury hotels must already be offering this service. However when I looked I discovered most weren't. I realised immediately that if we wanted an online gift voucher catalogue, then so must lots of other hotels in the UK. This is when the seed of SK Chase was born.

At the time I wasn't brave enough to set up on my own. I had a fantastic working relationship with my colleague, Stephanie Wilson, who was the revenue manager. I shared the idea with her while we were on a management course in Brussels and asked her if she wanted to come in on it with me 50/50. And she said 'Yes'!

Steph and I incorporated the business in August 2003 and started trading in June 2004. It took us ten months to build the first version of our gift voucher application. We launched with eight hotel clients, while continuing to work full time at The Town House Collection. Our first major breakthrough was when we secured The Gleneagles Hotel (two months after we launched). This was the point at which we knew the business was going to fly. We reckoned that if Gleneagles were keen to work with us, then it would only be a matter of time before other high profile hotels and resorts would feel the same way.'

So what do they do?

'We provide a service that enables our hotel clients to create, promote and sell their own range of gift experiences via their own branded gift voucher website (powered by SK Chase), which they link to from their own website. Each time a gift voucher is ordered, SK Chase issues and dispatches the gift voucher on behalf of the hotel.

We literally worked every single evening and Saturdays and Sundays. It was one of the most exciting periods in my life. We had a massive boost when Peter Taylor, the owner and Chair of The Town House Company (our previous employer) and who had supported our business from the very outset, offered a small office in the attic in one of his hotels rent free.

In December 2005 we employed our first member of staff, Natasha Lynn, who is still with us today and has blossomed with the company.'

What is the USP?

'Also, I realised that the reason the majority of luxury hotels hadn't implemented their own system is because there are a number of perceived barriers – a number of components required to set the system up. Gift vouchers aren't a hotel's core business, it's a fringe activity. Therefore they don't devote the same amount of time and resource to setting up sophisticated systems. Gift vouchers can also be perceived as a hassle to hotels due to the tracking and redemption. Therefore our experience is that hotels are delighted to outsource to SK Chase as it's a great way of generating extra sales revenue.'

How much planning did they do?

'In terms of business planning, we were forced to write a complete business plan, because we had applied for the Scottish Enterprise Tourism Innovation Award. A complete business plan, incorporating a marketing plan and full financial forecasts, was required.

This was a great exercise for Steph and I, and we actually both ended up enjoying the process. It really helped to crystallise our vision and how we thought we were going to achieve it.'

What start-up finance did they have?

'Steph and I didn't have any money at all! We ended up releasing equity on our own mortgages (I had a small flat in Leith at the time) and managed to secure £5k each. I remember having a conversation with my lender and explaining to them, very excitedly, that I was setting up my own business and wanted to release some equity on my mortgage. The woman I spoke to was really wonderful. She explained that they didn't lend on that basis (i.e., setting up businesses). Then she said, 'But of course, if you required a new car, then that would be within the rules'. And so, of course, I said that I also wanted a new car!

Peter Taylor lent us £5k and then we got a further £10k from Scottish Enterprise, via the Tourism Innovation Development Award. So we had a grand total of £25k start up capital.

This, however, was not sufficient to do everything we wanted to do (in five years we've invested over £200k in our software development). To get the first version of our software built we did a deal with a local software company; we offered them share-options in return for giving us a discounted software development rate.'

What other help and support did they receive?

'We received tons of support. In Scotland there are so many opportunities for assistance for new businesses; particularly those that have an innovative idea, which is scalable and with high ambitions, which we had and still have today. Support came from the Edinburgh Chamber of Commerce, where our adviser really helped us to understand the core strengths of our business model; and from Scottish Enterprise.

Our families too were great. My husband is an entrepreneur, and my mum was too. They have both really supported me.'

How has the business developed?

'While we process over £8m of gift voucher sales via our bank account, our actual turnover is £620,000. We employ five full-time and one part-time member of staff. 2009 was the first year we made a good profit.

We outsource our gift voucher fulfilment to a third party (a company that rents a warehouse on our behalf and employs staff to print and dispatch each gift voucher). We also outsource our software development company to our technology partner, Ezone Software.

Since the start in the attic we have moved office four times and grew our work force to nine members of staff. More recently we down-sized to five, with one part-timer, due to us restructuring and outsourcing the fulfilment of our gift vouchers.

We now provide our service to 285 hotels and resorts throughout the UK including The Ritz Hotel in London, De Vere Hotels, Elite Hotels, Celtic Manor and Rocco Forte Collection.'

What has been your biggest challenge?
'The recession shone a bright light on the problems within our business that Steph and I hadn't fully acknowledged. While from the outside the business looked like it was performing well and growing year on year, there were some internal issues that we hadn't addressed due to the fear of what the outcome would be.

We made some financial mistakes which we recognised a couple of years afterwards, so we then put a plan in place to rectify them. The recession put extra pressure on the business and forced Steph and I to address the core problems in a much deeper and quicker way.

It was one of the most painful experiences I've had since setting up the business. We made big and radical decisions in a very short space of time and had to make redundancies. These people had become our friends and I felt a huge sense of responsibility and sadness at having to let them go.

The key thing is, though, that the business is now in a stronger and more streamlined and efficient position than it was before this experience. So I can honestly say that in retrospect I'm glad it happened because I learnt so much more about business and what things are important. I am now in a position to prevent those things from happening again.'

CHAPTER FIFTEEN

MARKET RESEARCH

Many small businesses start up with little or no formal market research. You are often familiar with the product or market and can launch on instinct and optimism.

It might work out . . .

❝ *(We did) very little research, apart from looking at quite a few luxury hotel websites to identify whether they already offered an online gift voucher service. The idea was a gut thing and I knew it would work. When I shared the idea with hoteliers, they were very positive, so this reinforced my belief that we'd come across a winner.* ❞

Kaye Taylor, SK Chase

Or it might not . . .

❝ *It probably would have been sensible if I had thought to do some more market research at the time. I may not have set up, in fact, had I done this. Unfortunately I did not do enough research; hey ho retrospect is a wonderful thing!* ❞

Sally MacMillan, Ask Sally

What does market research tell you?

- Data about your market place (i.e., statistics and reports).
- Customer patterns and behaviour (i.e., field reports, market research).
- Customer needs (i.e., focus groups).
- What people think of your product, perhaps against competitors' (i.e., testing).
- What the competition is offering and how well it is doing (i.e., competitor analysis).

Research can be quantitative (numbers) or qualitative (descriptive; views or reactions). The bigger your proposed venture, the more advisable it is to commission market research (see Appendix).

If you are a doubter, don't think market research will take six months, cost thousands of pounds and come back with inconclusive results. Most likely, you will have already carried out some research in formulating your ideas, even if you didn't realise it. If you need finance to get going, you will need some kind of evidence that a market for your product exists. And even if not, don't you want to put your own investment of money and time on a sounder footing?

❛ *I decided that mums shopping online were my target market so I created a survey using Survey Monkey and my local Netmums very kindly agreed to run the survey as a competition (thanks Netmums!).*

I found out that mothers shopping online tended to favour "funky" and bright designs. I also discovered what they thought about green issues and what was most important to them as customers. It was very helpful both in planning the website and in building my business plan and I think having detailed market research helped me get my start up loan from Deutsche Bank. ❜

Tabitha Harman, Mimimyne

Get down and dirty with your market

Doing your research: Get to know your market and competitors

Research can be the key that unlocks business success. Find out as much as you can about your market and competition. Think about:

■ What more can you do to gain insight into the market?
■ Is it growing? Or changing?
■ How much competition will you face?
■ Has anyone else already developed your idea?
■ How does your idea differ from your competitors?
■ What are they charging? What don't they do very well?
(Source: www.barclays.co.uk/business (Go to 'Starting a business, tips, research'.))

If you are not looking for comprehensive market data or a large study of your potential purchasers, you can at least carry out your own research. It will give you valuable information and could well bring in some enquiries or interest. Let's take a couple of examples.

Face painting

If you have children, you'll go to birthday parties and fairs. If not, tag along with family and friends to their outings. Observe:

- who is offering face painting
- the price
- the range of faces/patterns offered
- how good they are/how long they take
- then read any leaflets or websites they have.

If you can get talking to them, ask them how much time they spend a week doing this, if they trained or got it from a book, how far they travel. Talk to the host afterwards and ask why she chose that person. Also look at family information magazines and websites to make sure the market isn't saturated.

You might come to the conclusion that birthday parties are a better bet because the host will pay you a fixed fee and you can leave once all the little darlings are done!

You might find that getting a concession, such as at a children's farm, does well. And what about taking a photo afterwards (to be emailed on) for a little bit more?

Your research can give you ideas or modify your product.

Now something more complex:

Corporate website design

For this you would really want to know what the competition was and what makes you stand out from it. This is a more difficult proposition because companies can get their websites designed anywhere in the world. They don't have to meet the designer in person, so in theory there's no geographic territory. Before you do your research, therefore, you would want to think whether you can choose a type of business (segment) more receptive to your approach.

Perhaps you decide on small start-ups. There is a good chance that these people would like their designer to be local and to be able to meet now and then. You might want to find out:

- what a new business pays on average for their website
- the kinds of needs – e-commerce, online brochure/contact details, provide information
- who would be commissioning you – are they design minded, techie, busy, fussy?

- how long they take to complete and sign off
- what backup they require
- that they can pay what you would like.

You could do this by:

- contacting your local Chamber of Commerce or the Federation of Small Businesses to see if any research or surveys have been conducted on commissioning websites; look at what information they give out to entrepreneurs for hiring a designer;

- networking and asking people about their website experience; why not ask one or two people if you could meet or phone them to discuss it in more depth; look at their website and have some questions to ask;

- search for or look up the websites of any competitors you come across; what are their key messages (price, design, technical know-how, backup, search engine know-how?); if you meet any of them, they might be friendly enough to share some information (don't assume this though!);

- offer a couple of guinea pigs a reduced rate website if you can ask them questions about what they want from a designer, and about the process afterwards.

The most valuable thing is to talk to people who might buy your product (target market). Lots of people will give their time for free to answer questions or you could offer a gift or free product. Make sure you write answers down, or record them, and write them up afterwards. Really learn from them and build them into your plans, even if this means making changes.

CHAPTER SIXTEEN

THE BUSINESS PLAN

Why do we hate doing the business plan?

No! Don't skip this bit! There are no official figures but from the businesses featured in this book it seems that a lot of women setting up a small business do not create a business plan. Men are probably no different. It's only if you are applying for start-up capital that you will have to do one.

Why don't people do one?

- I know what I'm going to do
- I haven't got the time
- I've got business in already
- I don't like figures
- I don't need a plan to tell me this will work
- I'm an instinctive kind of person.

You may have had sleepless nights about the uncertainty and challenge of the venture. Now you have got the courage to start, you don't want anyone or anything to tell you it won't work!

Why do you need to write a business plan?

The simple reason for a business plan is that it tells others what you intend to do. However, it is equally as good a document for you as the business owner. If you were setting off on a long car journey you would, *presumably*, check where you intend to get to; work out your route (and possibly revise it if you meet problems); make sure the car is roadworthy; and have your phone and provisions. Your venture should be seen in the same way.

A plan needn't take weeks to do and it could be prepared as part of your research phase.

It's very easy to get caught up in the enthusiasm, excitement and all the set-up tasks of a new business. This is the chance to pause, pull the results of your research together and really challenge your ideas. And if things need changing or tweaking, now is the time to do it. It's probably the first time you will have written down formally what you plan to do.

❝ *A business plan is a written document that describes a business, its objectives, its strategies, the market it is in and its financial forecasts. It has many functions, from securing external funding to measuring success within your business.* ❞

Business Link Website, *Prepare a business plan*

It is a business document, but you can still write it inspiringly. It needn't be stuffy. Writing down what, why, where, who, when and how, you'll be surprised how this can boost your confidence and validate your ideas.

❝ *At the beginning we worked with Business Link and attended a couple of free seminars targeting new businesses. As a result we were given a £500 loan on the basis that we came up with a business plan (which was all new to us) and they helped us along the way. However, we didn't do any real financial projections, just made a couple of guesses. In hindsight, I wish we'd been more financially 'savvy'. We wasted a lot of money in the first 18 months.* ❞

Nikki Geddes, Kiddy Cook Franchising

What's in a plan?

If you are starting up on your own, it can be quite simple. If you are daunted by the financial aspects, help is at hand. Your accountant, your bank's small business adviser or Business Link online can help. Check in case advisers charge.

Section in plan	What it is
An executive summary.	An overview of your business plans.
A short description of the business opportunity.	Who you are, what you plan to sell or offer, why and to whom.
The marketing and sales strategy.	Why people will buy and how you plan to reach them.
The management team and personnel.	Your CV plus those of any other key directors, advisers or personnel, with the emphasis on skills and experience.

The operations.	Your premises, production facilities, your management information systems and IT.
Financial forecasts.	All these plans in numbers.

(Source: Business Link Website, *Prepare a Business Plan*)

You can download a blank business plan, with guidelines, from the Business Link Website (at the time of going to press). Information is also available from banks. If you get help in completing it you will still, of course, have to supply the details; so you have to do your homework first.

Create a strategic plan

TRY THIS

Use your research to create a clear and honest set of Strengths, Weaknesses, Opportunities and Threats, or SWOT analysis. It's a good place to start for most business plans.

Strengths	Weaknesses
Fill in your strengths, those of your idea or workforce.	Write down your weaknesses or areas where your business might be exposed.
Opportunities	**Threats**
Think about the factors that will define the success of your business.	Go through all the potential threats to your business.

Spend time thinking about how you're going to address each of these areas. Build your decisions into your plan and back them up with strategies for success.
(Source: www.barclays.co.uk/business Go to 'Starting a business, tips, research')

❝ The Prince's Trust helped me do some planning, and my step-father is an accountant so he helped me with figures. But I didn't work it out to the last penny. If I had, I'd have probably walked away at the beginning! But things have worked out fine. ❞

Lorna Knapman, Love Food Festival

Work out the numbers

If you don't have spreadsheet skills then take a training course; you may be eligible for free training. Even if you've avoided numbers so far in your life, this is the time to grasp the nettle: the financial forecast is the heart of the business. Start off with money out (Outgoings) and money in (Income), and take each one in turn.

Let's look at a simple example: setting up Ally's Admin, a business offering business administration services. It starts in January with a small rented office (rates, heating etc. all in); a full time director (Ally) and a part-time employee. It is not registered for VAT yet.

Outgoings

Purchase of computer and printer	£1,200 to be paid in February
Purchase of stationery supplies	£500, in January and June
IT support	£150 a month
Rental of office	£600 per month
Wages	£1,000 per month (gross)
Advertising	£700 per quarter
Setting up website	£800, payable in February
Director's salary	£500 per month (increasing to £1,500 after six months' trading)

Ally's Admin Outgoings Year 1 (see Excel Table 1)

These can be forecast quite accurately, although cost control has to be kept tight. It would be prudent to add some contingencies, say, £300 a month.

Ally's Admin Income Year 1 (see Excel Table 2)

What do you think you'll get in? How quickly will you be paid? Let's say this company has good prospects:

Charging clients £500 a month, billing at the beginning of the month, with 30 days' payment terms. It starts with one client in March and gains one more client every two months. In December it ends the contracts with two clients but gains a new client on £1,000 a month. This assumes payment on time with no bad debts.

Excel Table 1 Ally's Admin Outgoings Year 1

	Jan	Feb	Mar	Apr	May	Jun	Jul	Aug	Sep	Oct	Nov	Dec	Total
IT equipment		1200											1200
Stationery	500					500							1000
IT support	150	150	150	150	150	150	150	150	150	150	150	150	1800
Office rental	600	600	600	600	600	600	600	600	600	600	600	600	7200
Wages	1000	1000	1000	1000	1000	1000	1000	1000	1000	1000	1000	1000	12000
Advertising		700			700			700			700		2800
Website		800											800
Salary	500	500	500	500	500	500	1500	1500	1500	1500	1500	1500	12000
Contingencies	300	300	300	300	300	300	300	300	300	300	300	300	3600
Total	3050	5250	2550	2550	3250	3050	3550	4250	3550	3550	4250	3550	42400

Excel Table 2 Ally's Admin Income Year 1

	Jan	Feb	Mar	Apr	May	Jun	Jul	Aug	Sep	Oct	Nov	Dec	Total
Client 1			500	500	500	500	500	500	500	500	500	500	5000
Client 2					500	500	500	500	500	500	500		3500
Client 3							500	500	500	500	500	500	3000
Client 4									500	500	500		1500
Client 5											500	500	1000
Client 6												1000	1000
Total	0	0	500	500	1000	1000	1500	1500	2000	2000	2500	2500	15000

Excel Table 3 Ally's Admin Profit and Loss Year 1

	Jan	Feb	Mar	Apr	May	Jun	Jul	Aug	Sept	Oct	Nov	Dec	Total
Income	0	0	500	500	1000	1000	1500	1500	2000	2000	2500	2500	15000
Outgoings	3050	5250	2550	2550	3250	3050	3550	4250	3550	3550	4250	3550	42400
Profit/loss	−3050	−5250	−2050	−2050	−2250	−2050	−2050	−2750	−1550	−1550	−1750	−1050	−27400

Ally's Profit/loss Year 1 (see Excel Table 3)

It shows that income isn't forecast to cover outgoings in Year 1 and it will need finance of just under £30,000 to get through. To reduce this, the director might reconsider hiring a part-time employee until Year 2. And she might be able to survive personally on less income; say just £6,000. This would reduce the forecast deficit to £9,400.

The joy of spreadsheets like Excel, is that you can play around with the numbers to see what happens to the bottom line. Of course, the numbers need to be based on reality. You can do three versions: optimistic, middle-of-the-road and doom-laden. The more research you conduct, the more accurate your input figures can be.

Alternative plans could be to start the business at home and increase the advertising; or adding other marketing and sales activity to see the income build up healthily towards the end of the year, enabling the business to expand.

If the director wanted to stick with the original forecast and went to a bank or another lender asking for £30,000 funding for Year 1, she would need to provide five years' of forecasts showing how sales will build up (backed up with a Marketing and Sales plan). The loan repayment would need to be built into the forecast, which would further reduce profits (but can be offset against tax).

And finally, some women do their business plan with aplomb!

> ❝ A business plan was written, which actually won an award as it had all the right elements of a winning idea and the know-how to make it work. ❞
>
> Yana Johnson MBE, Yana Cosmetics

CHAPTER SEVENTEEN

TAKE A STEP BACK

Does your business fit you?

By this stage you are well along in your plans for your work or business. A small idea may have grown into something more ambitious. Or you might have met a potential partner or adviser who suggests doing things differently. This chapter enables you to take a brief step back to see where you are and if things still fit into your life.

TRY THIS

Checklist, matching your plans with your abilities and lifestyle needs. You can probably think of more areas to focus on:

Area of focus	Questions to ask	Action
Your skills	Do you have the technical know-how or skills required, plus the organisational and financial abilities a business demands?	Get technical training or attend a business start-up course
Start-up demands	Are you able to do everything yourself (i.e., research, marketing, production/ ordering, delivery, IT etc.)? Will you use suppliers or staff?	Build a group of trusted suppliers who will follow your instructions (or advise you) at a reasonable price. Learn about employing people.
Workplace	If setting up at home, do you have the right space and privacy for your business? Or do you need to find a commercial property?	Allocate a room, clear a garage or cellar, erect a garden office. Check if you need to pay business rates. Research commercial property.
Work/life balance	Does this fit in time-wise and emotionally with your family or other commitments?	Discuss it with all concerned. Ensure back up childcare and cancel social life for at least a year!

Money	Are you investing enough to get the venture off the ground? Do you have enough to live on if you don't make money at first?	Get your personal finances in order and do some financial planning, with an adviser if necessary.
Personality	You may work alone all day; you may have to stand for hours at a stall, encouraging people to come over; you may need to spend a lot of time with clients individually; you may need to sell by telephone. What does your business require and are you suited to it?	Reflect on this; talk to people who know you well; take a personality test; do assertiveness training or coaching. Be aware of how you come across to people.

Personality is key

The last aspect is really important, especially in a service or direct-selling business. People are more likely to want to buy from a cheerful person who is interested in them, than from a moaner or a self-absorbed person. Have a range of persona from professional to bubbly, to suit each client, but always be friendly. Also learn to take feedback or criticism without getting defensive.

How often do you go into independent shops to find the owners ignore you? Or even look at you as if you are a nuisance? And how often do they handle complaints or returns poorly? Learn from other people's demeanour and think how they could do better business if they just smiled.

CHAPTER EIGHTEEN

RAISING FINANCE

Why do we see this as a barrier?

❝ Finance has long been regarded as the main obstacle preventing women from starting and growing a successful business. Although the sources of finance are common to women and men, women perceive higher access barriers. ❞

Professor Sara Carter, *Women's Enterprise and Access to Finance*[7]

Now, this is interesting! It is commonly thought that the banking sector discriminates against female business start-ups. However, this report has found that the evidence of 'supply-side discrimination . . . is rather weak', while, 'in terms of demand-side debt aversion . . . there is a stronger case.'

In other words, we don't like going to the bank to borrow money. But perhaps the following will change your mind:

❝ . . . women succeed at or above the rates of men when seeking bank finance, which is a major encouragement to women thinking of starting up in business in this challenging climate. It also finds that women are less likely than men to have been rejected due to poor business planning, and are less likely to have been unable to make a repayment on loans, suggesting that women can be better at managing their business finances. ❞

Press release, *Myths and Realities of Women's Access to Finance*,
Women's Enterprise Task Force[8]

And yet, women are less likely to apply for financing outside of their family, and when they do, they ask for less money than men.

So this goes back to the ambition we have talked about earlier. There are women with oodles of confidence and optimism about their business, who have later admitted they did not think big enough when it came to funding their start-up. Is this about taking ourselves seriously, our attitude to money and debt or just not doing our figures properly?

❛ *Interestingly, when we entered the Tourism Innovation Development Award to apply for matched funding, we only applied for £5k. However when we discovered we had won, the judges explained that they wanted to grant £10k as they thought we had underestimated the amount required. And they were right!*

We had a grand total of £25k start-up capital. However, this still was not sufficient to do everything we wanted to do . . . and in fact over the five years we've been trading we've invested over £200k in our software development.

For me it boiled down to not feeling comfortable asking for more money, which essentially comes down to how much I valued myself (at the time). It's taken a few years for me to realise just how worthy I am! Now I would feel much more confident applying for funding. And I would consider myself deserving. Back then I knew I had a fantastic idea, and I truly believed in it, but I didn't feel so confident about asking for funds. ❜

Kaye Taylor, SK Chase

Sources of finance

Self-funding
- personal/family money
- from sales, little up-front investment.

Debt/grants
- bank overdraft
- credit cards
- bank loan
- remortgaging
- loans from friends/colleagues
- grants/community funding.

Factoring (to help cashflow)
- asset and invoice factoring.

Equity (giving up a share of the business)
- family and friends buy a share
- business angels
- venture capital
- private equity.

❛ *The most common means of finance for both men and women are current accounts, bank overdrafts, credit cards and deposit accounts. Women are more likely to use personal finance, family members and other employment to fund start-up.* ❜

❛ *Women may actually be more likely to get free banking because their business is smaller, but if they have a term loan, as women tend to borrow smaller sums, they may have higher administrative charges.* ❜

❛ *Capitalisation for women-led businesses is one-third the levels of capitalisation used by male-owned businesses. The mean total starting capital of male-owned firms was £18,683. The equivalent figure for women-led firms is £6,433.* ❜ [9]

❛ *Women-owned businesses start with lower levels of capitalisation, use lower levels of debt finance, and are much less likely to use formal and informal venture capital. Importantly, initial under-capitalisation has a long-term negative effect on business survival and growth.* ❜

Some other findings from *Women's Enterprise and Access to Finance*

What is the best route for you?

Each business and owner is different so there is no single best route. But some points are worth noting:

■ Look into the grants available. These can be by region, gender, ethnicity, disability, sector, age, for training or employing people; and no doubt other categories. They can take some researching, but your bank or Business Link online might be able to advise you on what's available and your eligibility. If you don't apply, you won't get it.

■ Keep credit card finance to short-term needs, and not beyond a few thousand pounds. Beyond that it would work out more expensive than other forms of loan.

■ Borrowing from friends and family is common and can work. Make sure both parties have the same understanding as to the purpose and repayment terms. If interest is paid, there are tax implications for both. Ideally, an agreement should be in writing to reduce the possibility of misunderstandings or arguments. As with issuing shares to friends and family, it would be advisable for both parties to get legal and/or financial advice.

■ Government schemes might be suitable for you. Check what is available at the time of reading.

■ If your cashflow needs a helping hand, and you are not paid up-front, then look at how quickly invoices are paid. If wringing payment out of clients is a problem, consider invoice factoring. Put simply, a third party takes on your creditors, paying you the majority of your outstanding invoices, for a percentage.

■ In a recession even good ideas get turned down for finance. But bear in mind, that if someone refuses you funding, they are giving you useful feedback on the potential of your idea. This may be because your figures aren't presented well enough. Or that you haven't properly evidenced, or have been too optimistic about, your sales. You might not come across professional enough for them to have confidence in you, especially if they ask you questions and you can't find the right figures for the answer.

Of course, there are differences between lenders, and sometimes perseverance can pay off:

❝ *I had a very clear idea of projections and wasn't overzealous. In March 2009 I approached NatWest for a Business Enterprise loan and was declined because we hadn't invested enough of our own money. I applied to Barclays and was accepted with the same business plan. My advice: "Don't give up".* ❞

Cherry Parsons, CJ Motor Repairs Ltd

And if you still have doubts about funding:

❝ *What I would say to a woman in a similar position is to think about the idea you have, and then imagine that a really successful man or woman you know had the same idea. Then consider whether you'd be willing to invest in their idea and them. If the answer is 'Yes', then how much would you be willing to invest (assuming you had plenty of money available)? This is the amount you should be asking for!* ❞

Kaye Taylor, SK Chase

CHAPTER NINETEEN

THE SERIOUS STUFF: FOR BUSINESS

Setting up your business

Take a deep breath, because there are a lot of boxes to tick in setting up and running even a small business. You must follow up every section yourself as it will vary according to your business. Contacts and information are in the Appendix.

Legal status

See Chapter 6 for a discussion of sole trader, limited company, partnership and other structures. If you are setting up a small business, you will most likely choose a limited company, or partnership if you have colleagues involved on an equal basis. But there are also structures for businesses with different values and contractual arrangements, such as franchises and social enterprises (Chapter 27).

The business was set up as a sole trader and then quickly changed status to limited liability. This was for practical reasons: when the business grew and changed in its status and operations, then so did I. It enabled me to make clear decisions about the way forward and gave me ample control within that decision-making process.

Yana Johnson, MBE, Yana Cosmetics Ltd

We set up as a limited company; we didn't consider any other options. In fact we didn't even get a lawyer involved, we just downloaded the relevant forms from the Companies House website and completed them the way we thought best! I've realised in retrospect that so much of what we did at the beginning was due to naivety, but this isn't always a bad thing. When you aren't aware of how things are done, your mind always comes up with new ways of doing them, it challenges the system.

We've since had a lawyer make changes to our articles of association, particularly as we have share option holders and one other shareholder.

Kaye Taylor, SK Chase Ltd

The structure you choose will affect:

- the tax and National Insurance that you pay
- the records and accounts that you have to keep
- your financial liability if the business runs into trouble
- the ways your business can raise money
- the way management decisions are made about the business

(Source: Business Link website, *Legal Structures*)

❝ *I set up as a limited company but I have since changed to being a sole trader as it is easier to deal with. I could have saved myself some money.* ❞
Charlotte Carr, franchisee, Kiddy Cook

Find the right adviser

Many small businesses set up without advisers, so you need to ask, 'What can this person add to my business?' Then look at their cost and what fees you can negotiate.

Accountant

- Companies with a turnover of less that £6.5 million and starting up after April 2008 do not need an annual audit of accounts.

- A limited company or limited liability partnership must file annual accounts with Companies House. An accountant can produce these accounts for you. If you are not confident with figures or don't have the time, this can be worthwhile outsourcing (although you must always understand and know the financial state of your business).

- You may need financial advice as your business launches and develops. You will certainly benefit from tax and pensions advice.

- If you have to register for VAT (check HMRC website) or run a payroll for employees, an accountant or bookkeeper can do this for you.

Lawyer

- Registering a limited company and agreements between directors/partners.
- Becoming a franchisee and buying a business.

- Contracts with clients and suppliers.
- Employment contracts.
- Terms of business or conditions of sale.
- Debt recovery.
- Property transactions.
- Intellectual property.
- Litigation.

Coach, adviser or mentor

If you find the right person, experienced in the start-up sector, this person can be worth their weight in gold. Don't commit to a long-term contract until you know you get on with this person and can get value from them. It can be beneficial to step outside of close family and friends and get an objective viewpoint. A coach does not give advice, but guides and brings out the inspiration and confidence in you to take the business forward.

> *I used a business coach and signed up for her Business Accelerator Course. She has a wealth of experience and has been there and done it. As I work on my own, it's great to be able to tap into this knowledge and it's partly because of this support that I've been able to move the business forward. And do it quite quickly.*

Samantha Russell, Sardine Web Design

> *Business Link was invaluable for starting up, with courses, mentoring and information.*

Corinne McLavy, Zero3 Marketing

Getting commercial property

Finding the right business property can take a long time especially if you have specific requirements. Shops might be easier to find in a downturn but they must be in the right location. Consider the following.

- Location (for you, customers/clients and employees).
- Rateable value as well as rent/mortgage payments.
- Check rent or rate increases in future years.
- Your specific requirements (space, parking, client privacy, equipment, water, electricity, workshop, etc.).
- Disability access (legally required for staff and customers).
- Health and safety requirements (if buying, get a structural survey, just as you

would a home).
■ Make sure all costs are built into your financial plan.

Commercial property agents operate like residential ones (they are sometimes under the same roof) and there are also property search specialists who can look for your specific property. Check whether they charge an up-front fee.

Guard your intellectual property

❛ *Intellectual Property was my greatest problem. Designs being ripped off and sold overseas is no fun; pursuing international copyright law is a bit out of my financial league. My greatest threat is that someone will do what I do better and cheaper.* ❜

Lisa Cole, Lactivist

This area covers your ideas and inventions and what protection is available against copying and theft. It's not easy, as copies of a product or design can spread quickly to market stalls or through the web. Protecting ideas is a real grey area; you can pitch for business, for instance, and not be selected, but see one of your ideas (or something close) appear months later. Proving it was your idea originally is difficult. Real protection and enforcement is expensive.

Laws that protect you
■ *Patent protection*: For inventions.
■ *Copyright*: For creative work.
■ *Design right and registration*: For product characteristics.
■ *Trade marks*: Signs, symbols, logos, words, sounds or music (such as jingles) that distinguish your products and services from those of your competitors.
(Source: Business Link website, *Protecting your intellectual property*)

❛ *The greatest challenge that we faced was to our trade mark. After applying for registration, another music group tried to register a mark with a similar name. We pointed out our prior use and the dangers of operating with a similar name, but this rival group nevertheless tried to block the progress of the registration. Unfortunately we had to incur legal costs but ultimately won.* ❜

Karen Sherr, Musical Minis

Untangle the regulations

❛...respondents reported that "increased regulation" was the most important barrier to the business meeting its objectives over the previous two years. This came ahead of other factors such as obtaining finance or having adequately trained staff...❜

Putting the economy back on track: Work-Life Balance, FSB[10]

Business complains about red tape, and governments vow to get off their backs. However, there will always be regulations and legislation, much of it for good reason. Employees and customers need to be protected from unscrupulous traders and if you, as a business, have the right policies and procedures, you are less likely to be taken to court.

Each industry has different regulations; you must do your homework and get proper advice. Similarly, you need to be aware of basics such as contract law.

TRY THIS

Here are some other major areas to look into:

Legislation/regulation	What is it?
Health and safety	Legislation governing your premises and your products. Essential for food and catering businesses as well as nurseries and childminders. Even if you work from home, if clients or others visit and have an accident it is your responsibility. Insurance covers you for this, but it's better to do a safety check first.
Environment and climate change	Again, mostly for businesses with production facilities. But a 'green audit' would look at your use of resources and energy whatever your size, and publicising a low carbon footprint is something many consumers respond positively to.
Employment	Employees are entitled to a safe environment to work in and protection from discrimination and unfair dismissal. There

	is much legislation covering employment (including parental leave). See Chapter 21.
Disability discrimination	This relates to employment and property access, but can still affect the self employed. If, say, you are a coach or counsellor working from a third floor office or flat, you ought to have a lift for wheelchair access (or offer an alternative location).
Selling, advertising and digital marketing	Including European directives protecting customers of door-to-door and market stall sellers, and mail order and internet selling.
Working time directive	European directive limiting working hours of employees.
Licensing	Covering the sale of alcohol.
Advertising standards	What you can and cannot say and do in ads; product claims

Compliance costs must be forecast and built into your financial plans. The risk of non-compliance and consequent accidents, litigation or charges is far more damaging. See also the Appendix.

CHAPTER TWENTY

MARKETING

A more complex plan

We've looked in Part 2 at a marketing plan for an individual. A programme for a business can contain much of this activity, but it needs to be more complex. A trading business needs to broadcast its message more widely (whether or not you meet your customers) and branding comes into play. Before you plan your marketing, however, you need to know what you are aiming for.

Working out the numbers

Forecast sales need to be calculated as part of your homework, along with pricing. This requires research, (commissioned market research if you are aiming big); testing, if you can; and financial planning, with an adviser if you don't have the expertise (see Chapter 19).

So what is your strategy regarding market potential? Are you so ambitious you want to be market leader? Would you prefer to be a niche player? Or will you get going with a certain level of stock and see how it goes? Whichever route you choose, let's look at sales growth.

How can you build sales?

Make it popular

Have a product for which there is a **big demand**. If it's a once-in-a-lifetime purchase, you need to continually attract lots of customers. If it's a repeat purchase, you have to build loyal purchasers. So how are you going to be more attractive than the competition?

Make it desirable

Set a **higher**, or **premium price**. You will need to have evidence that a profitable market exists at this level. You will therefore have to have a quality product and the marketing must project the right image.

And after your initial success:

Diversify

Alternatively, you can **develop new products**, ideally to the same market-place. That way you don't have to learn about a new set of people and start marketing to them from scratch. If everyone thinks your summer dresses are fantastic, the chances are they will also flock to your winter woollies, as long as your branding is consistent.

Increase the territory

You can increase your geographic reach (and thus market) by enlisting **others to sell for you**. This would entail an incentivised sales force, direct selling distributors or franchises (Chapter 27).

Develop your marketing strategy

So far you have researched the market and have forecast your sales potential (which your supply or production must meet) and set your price. What must your marketing do?

Successful marketing is meeting the expectations and needs of your customers. Some people aim to surpass the expectations, but there's no need to get carried away. It is about building relationships (not necessarily face to face), knowing the benefits of your product and communicating to your audience.

The marketing plan

Section	Content
Introduction	'This Marketing Plan will…'.
A summary of your business aims	Copy from your Business Plan.
SWOT analysis (see Barclays information above)	This stands for Strengths, Weaknesses (internal analysis), Opportunities and Threats (externals analysis). In an an ideal world all your strengths would match opportunities! Be honest about your weaknesses; threats are always there because the market changes. It's a useful exercise getting you to think more about your market and your plans.
Marketing objectives	In current jargon, these should be SMART: **S**pecific – put numbers to it

	Measurable – so you know when you've reached it
	Achievable – within resources and confines of market
	Realistic – within your capability
	Timed – put a deadline for every objective
Tactics	How you will achieve your objectives? Select the right mix of communications for your audience (see below).
Budgeted	Purchase diligently and spend only what you have planned to.
Evaluation	What worked? What didn't? Feed it back in to revise plan.

The plan should answer these questions:

What. . .	. . . is the product or service?
	. . . is needed to achieve targets?
Who. . .	. . . will buy it?
	. . . will implement the marketing plan?
Why. . .	. . . should someone buy it?
	. . . buy it from you?
How. . .	. . . will you communicate to your target audience?
When. . .	. . . will you start selling?
	. . . will you know you have achieved your objectives?
Where. . .	. . . will you sell it?

Think about the four Ps

A simple way to start marketing is to think in terms of the four Ps: product, place, price, promotion

Product
Describe this in terms of customer value, the benefits it provides. What is your unique selling proposition (USP)?

Place
This traditionally meant the distribution channel, envisaging a product that went to a shop, or was bought from a direct response advertisement. Now, of course, it includes direct selling and internet selling.

Price

Determined by competitor pricing, your costs and positioning (perceived value).

Promotion

The activity or tactics you carry out to create awareness of your product, persuade people to try or buy it.

Create your marketing mix

TRY THIS

Advertising

- The advertising industry has changed drastically in the last few years. It has been doubly affected by recession and the internet, which is now starting to be a serious medium for advertisers. So think beyond just print and broadcast.
- Some products (especially brands) need big advertising budgets and some sell only by direct response ads (look at the weekend supplements).
- Advertising for the small business can be very expensive. You need to know: does it reach my audience without much wastage and does it work? Sometimes the last question is answered only by trial.
- If advertising is important to your product it is worth hiring an agency to do creative work and media buying.

Public relations

- Most commonly, PR is getting the press to talk positively about you or your product. If you have the time and the confidence, you can do this yourself: get to know which media reaches your audience and plan stories around your business and product. If your business grows, it could be a good investment to hire a PR agency with experience of your sector.
- A full PR plan will include all your stakeholders; for instance, a school visit, a report for investors, environmental information for a pressure group, a party for suppliers.
- Even if you are not an e-commerce business a website is now an expected communications channel. And social networking (Facebook, Twitter etc.) is rapidly turning commercial.

	• At the end of the day, though, all the 'chat' and publicity needs to be turned into sales. Build in some simple customer feedback to find out where they heard of your product.
Events	• At all events you need to think of your overall appearance: logo and 'corporate identity'; dress code or uniform of all personnel; product presentation. This can be sales events, exhibitions, networking, community events and social occasions. This isn't about just presenting your product; it communicates your ethos and values.
Social networking	• Still in its infancy, social networking, and its cousins Tweeting, blogging and texting, are principally intended for contact. However, they are beginning to be used as promotion and sales channels, which will no doubt annoy the purists who will go off and invent something else.

Karen Purves of the Centre for Effective Marketing is a fan of Twitter: 'What's great about Twitter is that you now have access to people who were previously unattainable. Twitter gives you an opportunity to learn about new things, come across new blogs etc. It has the potential of changing your information-gathering systems.'[11]

Your marketing mix will select those activities that best reach your target audience within your budget. Your marketing plan will combine your activities into a schedule. It should outline how you (and others) will carry it out, plus your key product benefits and messages. Each element should contain costs. And don't forget to evaluate and feed this back into the plan for the next year.

CHAPTER TWENTY ONE

EMPLOYING PEOPLE

Set things up correctly

The chances are, you will begin by employing one or two people in your business. You may be given all kinds of advice by fellow entrepreneurs about 'getting round' the regulations: hiring self-employed people; varying the hours; paying cash in hand.

Yes, many freelancers and contractors will be suitable for your business, and their roles won't justify employment. You must ensure that they are registered self employed (or are a limited company) or you might be liable for their income tax (see Chapter 7). However, some roles will develop as the business grows and employment makes sense. This is a big subject area that demands further study. But here are some pointers:

TRY THIS

Get reliable people and pay the market rate (or more).

Staff are what make your business as it grows; you want motivated people who want to succeed with you.

Have employment contracts drawn up by a lawyer and set up payroll systems properly.

Informal working and uncertainty demotivates and does not attract good people.

Know about employment law: sick pay and leave, discrimination laws, equal pay, grievance procedures, unfair dismissal, redundancy, parental leave (for starters).

There are companies, and some banks, which offer employment advice for a reasonable monthly payment. If you have only a few employees, this is worth looking into.

Have a job description and career plan for every employee: training and development.

Ask yourself, if you were in their shoes, what career progress would you want to make with the company?

An employer treads a difficult path, but if your philosophy is to offer the

Bean bags, pool tables and goldfish tanks may not be your style (and they're

best you can and expect their best in return you will reduce conflict and create efficiency.

Listen to your staff and incentivise creativity.

so 90s) but aim to provide a stimulating, rewarding environment.

They can come up with brilliant ideas that can develop your company.

CHAPTER TWENTY TWO

IF I KNEW THEN WHAT I KNOW NOW...

A chance to learn from others' experiences

This is where the going gets rough, so steel yourself. As a freelance, losing your living and having to return to employment is heartbreaking. But, as a bigger business, you carry more liability and risk. If things go wrong, you can come out not just losing your income but owing other people money or even being sued.

There are many pitfalls awaiting a new business and you should brainstorm what else may lurk round the corner for your venture. Here are three examples: when the sales don't meet target; when you are let down by your supplier; when you have a personal or domestic crisis.

'I was certain the market would be there!'

The lesson here is for the business set up on a wing and a prayer. You have this great idea because:

'I bought this fantastic kaftan in Marrakesh; I just know I could import them for the UK market.'

The kaftan is hardly a mass market item for the UK and to specialise in a single, niche market item is risky. Much better to sell a small range of Mediterranean-style clothes and accessories, with the kaftan as a key item. And avoid carrying too much stock.

'There's this brilliant new technique to teach people to ski. I'm buying my local franchise for £10,000.'

The ski instructor franchise might be brilliant for the sporty, but £10,000? How long would it take to earn your money back?

'I've made this to-die-for blackcurrant and egg white facepack and I just *know* everyone will love it!'

Ok, Anita Roddick started The Body Shop with a homemade product and shedloads of enthusiasm, but that was then (1970s). Today, the market is flooded with 'natural' toiletries and big names. You would have to be certain you had something original and a channel through which to market it.

Of course, these examples are tongue-in-cheek (and not typical of our case studies). But the point is that we can get bowled over with an idea or creation and not stop to consider – which means research – whether it's going to be viable.

We also have to be resilient and bounce back, even if it's a few years later.

‘ *I set up my first business in my early twenties but didn't really research my product very well and the sales did not come. So reluctantly I went back to work.* ’

Cari Parker, The Dales Party Company Ltd

And we need to adapt. What you sell, the way you deliver it, the price or fee you charge, all need to be flexible.

‘ *I was initially selling one-off modules of training – hour-long sessions of bespoke training for £35. I realised that I was going to have to get a lot of sessions to make any money. This was also not good for the learners as there was no follow up on their learning. I now offer training packages of a number of sessions, initial assessment and guides. This allows me to give a better solution and gives the clients something tangible to buy.* ’

Mary Thomas, Concise Training

'Where's my supplier gone?'

Everyone in business has to buy something: a computer, paper, raw materials, training, premises. We have to search for the best provider of these, and often pay up-front. So it's vital that we research suppliers too so that we know we are getting a good product and are not going to be ripped off. Networking can help give you contacts (although still no guarantee of quality) and word-of-mouth is even better.

‘ *I paid for a service on the internet that was supposed to put my products on a website that was really important for my product, but they failed to deliver.* ’

Lisa Cole, Lactivist

A few tips:

- Don't buy on price alone. Be prepared to pay at least mid-market price.

- Don't take on someone because they are nice or you 'click'.

- Do some research – the *Which?* guides for equipment, for instance. Search online for reviews and comparisons or get product magazines. Talk to people who have bought the product. You won't necessarily want the same as them but get their advice on how they chose that one.

- If you have a professional association or industry body, see if they have recommended suppliers. They may offer discounts too.

- Get referrals for services like consultancy and training. If they can't supply them, don't use them. Check referrals properly (see Case Study in Chapter 10).

- Make sure you consider a number of options or providers. Don't buy the first you come across.

If you think your business could be vulnerable to any kind of loss, theft or fraud, discuss it with your insurer. There may be a suitable product for you.

'Life keeps getting in the way'

Working was easy when my son was tiny; he was quite happy breastfeeding while I worked on the computer. It got more difficult as he got older and mobile and for a time almost impossible. He developed behavioural problems when I split up with his father and spent many days excluded from school. It is difficult to work when you are on call to collect your child from school. At one point I had to sit in the staff room in case of an incident. At this time I was designing websites so I would sit with my laptop and work. My son's behavioural problems put a halt to any PR for a year and the business suffered from that.

Lisa Cole, Lactivist

When crises happen, something has to give, and it can't be your children. If an emergency or illness happens and you don't have grandparents nearby, you need someone local, familiar to your children who can scoop them up. Set the boundaries of your work, but also allow yourself some childcare support as a safety net. That way, you will also be more focussed.

Celebrate your achievements

CASE STUDY

CJ Motor Repairs, run by Cherry Parsons, with her partner Jamie
www.cjmotorrepairs.co.uk
Business: Vehicle servicing, repairs and MOTs. Basic car maintenance courses

The story of Cherry's start up, in January 2009, is a harrowing one, containing many of life's challenges that would cause most people to buckle. She has worked out her USP and focused on it in textbook style. The business deserves to be a success, but instead she is fighting all the way:

'My father runs a garage in Southampton and I had worked for him for around 20 years, primarily doing the accounts, and running it for the eight years before we set up CJ Motor Repairs. I gained a vast amount of inside knowledge and was really concerned about the poor quality of work in the car repair business. Most weeks we had new customers who believed they had paid for full services when in fact very little had been done.

My father is, as you would say "old school". He didn't think customer relations were as important as I did. I was keen to run car maintenance courses to give our customers some knowledge and confidence and show them how to save money. As a woman in the trade, I found many of my female customers were relieved to be dealing with another woman.

I grew my father's business from a £90,000 turnover to a £350,000 turnover in four years without increasing staff, mainly through customer relations and time management. However, our future is uncertain as the landlord might not renew the lease and the property has planning permission. So five years ago I started looking for another site to accommodate my father's business. In February 2008, I found fabulous premises: already a garage kitted out with all the equipment and loads of room for us to grow. There were classrooms for me to run the courses and spare offices to rent out if we wanted, plus 13 allocated parking spaces I couldn't believe my luck!'

A difficult decision to take

'My dad was excited but when it came to the crunch he decided he didn't want to invest any money or move the garage. I was gutted. In a few years he would retire and the lease might end, so I had to make a decision for my family's future. I had got so excited about the changes I could make: finally everyone could come to our garage, knowing they could trust us 100% and learn how to save money.

My partner Jamie had the same vision, so we decided to go ahead without my dad. In between all of this I had been trying for a baby and, having said "Yes" to taking over the lease in February 2008, I found out I was pregnant in March. We were petrified but it felt right.

That year, during the pregnancy, I took no holiday so that I could save it for my maternity leave. However, one month before Skye was born we found out my father had prostate cancer. So I did all I could to support his business before mine opened.

We took on the lease at the same time as Sky was born, *and* the recession was on. So we didn't get going until the beginning of 2009.'

How did she finance the start-up?

'We tried all the banks, but, despite good personal credit ratings, they rejected us. We had no equity in the house, due to the slump in property prices.

So, although we hate borrowing money from family, my sister and her husband and Jamie's sister and her partner lent us the money to get going. My father refused, despite previously saying he would. Shortly afterwards we got a loan from Barclays.'

What preparation did she do for the startup?

'I used a NatWest business plan originally. I had a very clear idea of projections and wasn't overzealous. I hadn't worked with any adviser at this stage.

I felt, perhaps naively, my years of experience were sufficient research. I had listened to thousands of customers complaining how much cars cost to run and maintain so I believed they would come flocking! We have achieved 75% of my turnover projections on servicing, repairs and MOTs, but the courses have been disappointing.'

How did she cope with two businesses and a baby?
'I went back to work one week after Skye was born as no one else could do the accounts. I also took them home, although my time was limited with a new baby *and* planning the new business. I did all I physically could to support my dad. This caused some problems within our family unit as I was supposed to be resting after a particularly difficult birth; we had both been rushed off to intensive care. There was obviously a lot of stress, and the tiredness was overwhelming. I was driven by my belief in our potential and the need to make a difference.'

What other challenges have there been?
'We didn't foresee it but our greatest challenge was getting new customers and not being tarred with the same brush as all the other garages. With every effort to introduce ourselves and our fabulous new garage, we were too good to believe.

Another difficulty is our extortionate business rates (£1,500 a month). They are higher than other local business because we are on a trading estate. I know of another local garage with a £450,000 turnover that only pays £90 per month. I thought we would get a small business rates discount but our rateable value was too high. This, combined with the rent of a large building ready to house my father's business, was a strain for a completely new business. We nearly went under in the first few months; Barclays Bank was our saviour amidst this frustration.

Also, my father saw us as a threat and didn't help at all. I'm saddened by this and realise that my family loyalty was misplaced.'

What has been positive?
'I contacted Business Link in our second month and had meetings that helped me focus my goals and strategies. We also talked about marketing and growth. They are very professional, productive and enthusiastic.'

Where is she at the moment?
'The business is a real struggle right now, but I know from personal experience that I can come through this. It is very easy to get worn down by everyday life sometimes; we too easily forget how special we are or how far we have come.

Over Christmas my sister-in-law said, "Celebrate how far you have come, be proud of your achievements and the difference you are making." I felt like she had given me a lift back up.'

Summary checklist: Setting up a small business

✓ Make time to reflect on your motivation, ambition and attitude to risk.

✓ Challenge and test your idea as much as possible.

✓ Do as much market research as you can afford.

✓ Prepare a SWOT analysis.

✓ Prepare a business plan.

✓ Do your financial planning.

✓ Get help with these if needed.

✓ Step back and check your lifestyle works for this.

✓ Consider your self-image and approach to finance.

✓ Back your business with sufficient capital.

✓ Look into all the regulatory requirements.

✓ Don't skimp on professional advice.

✓ Develop a marketing strategy and written plan.

✓ Build in support and contingencies for crises.

Part 4:
Change of
Life Ventures

Introduction

This part focuses on times when women face challenge and change. For some, the challenge is to work round a young family. For others, it requires overcoming disadvantage. We will meet women who have taken life by the scruff of the neck and fought to set themselves up in business. As a result, they have reclaimed their self esteem and gained control of their lives.

For many of these women employment is ruled out by circumstances or discrimination. Family demands, disability, age (at both ends of the spectrum) or disadvantage mean that the traditional workplace does not see them as the ideal employee. That's the negative. But what is to be celebrated is that these groups of people are in the vanguard of the new entrepreneurs.

Here we will look at the diverse lives of the women who now work for themselves and the ways that they are doing it. We'll meet the new entrepreneurs, who mostly work from home:

■ the mumpreneur
■ the younger and older businesswomen
■ the rural-based
■ women with disability
■ other disadvantaged unemployed, homeless and ex-offender.

And we'll look at the different ways you can be in business today, e.g.:

■ direct selling distributor
■ franchisee
■ home-based business

- online trader
- social entrepreneur.

Could you be part of this revolution?

The nuts and bolts of setting up a business are just as relevant to these ventures, so see previous sections for these. Here, we will focus on the stories and the organisations that offer help to those people who need extra support in setting up their business.

CHAPTER TWENTY THREE

TURN CHALLENGE INTO OPPORTUNITY

When work doesn't work

This is very much a positive story, but we should briefly acknowledge that many people are self employed because the workplace has rejected them. Some women are treated badly at work when they become pregnant or return after maternity leave (we've heard from some of them in the case studies). Despite UK and European legislation, some employers just don't get it. In other circumstances, women hit the glass ceiling, which we've talked about earlier, or don't get equal treatment.

> ❛ In a male-dominated industry, women have to work differently, to earn respect, before the barriers come down. ❜
>
> Kavita Oberoi FRSA, founder and MD of Oberoi Consulting

Add to that, if you are over 50, disabled or have a less-than-conventional history, you are likely to come up against discrimination when applying for jobs. Disability discrimination, like sex discrimination, is outlawed, but employers regularly write off candidates over 50 – even 40. This is often such a waste of experience and talent.

Going through the experience of discrimination is unpleasant and knocks your self esteem. But, if you can come out of it with a resolve to work for yourself, you could have a wonderful opportunity ahead of you. And as you map out your plans for your new business, remind yourself that many people are employed in jobs wishing they weren't.

Consider the opportunities

These are endless, but here are some typical change of life businesses:

■ **Internet trading or networking**
The internet has revolutionised the lives of people who cannot, or don't want

to commute to a job. For instance, there are many websites for working and self employed mums and a wealth of trading sites for baby-related products – usually run by mums!

■ **Franchisee or direct selling distributor**

This has been a huge growth area. Again for new mums, carers or semi-retired people this is an opportunity to take on a ready-made business, possibly even a brand name, and sell in your local community.

■ **Childcare**

Childminders are often older women with a grown-up family. Some nannies are also self-employed, although many have been scooped into the PAYE net in recent years.

■ **Coaching or counselling**

These are two very common fields that women retrain for in mid-career. This may be because of redundancy, a career break or wanting to do something more caring.

■ **Ebay traders**

There are lots of people who have built a living around trading, although I wonder if their houses are filled with cardboard boxes and masking tape! The tax authorities sometimes catch up with those who are not properly registered as a business.

■ **The rural business**

Spurred on by the threats to farm incomes, many women have started businesses, some complementary to agriculture and some very different. These include holiday accommodation, educational visits, produce sale and small scale production.

■ **Social enterprise**

These are businesses with a primary purpose of benefiting the environment and/or the community. While they need to make a profit, this is mostly shared with poorer communities or ploughed back into the business. This isn't for you if you want to make a million.

Some businesses develop out of hobbies, so you can't quite tell when they turn serious. And some married women's earnings are low enough, to begin with at least, that they stay under their husband's tax return. In contrast, others can't make the first move before the red tape unwinds. Childminding, holiday accommodation and anything involving food are examples where you must work with a copy of the regulations in one hand from the beginning. Health and safety compliance, in particular, is vital to the success of your business.

CHAPTER TWENTY FOUR

HOME-BASED BUSINESSES: THE HIDDEN ENTREPRENEURS

Are you planning to work from home? Congratulations! You may be unseen, unheard and unsung, but you are part of a new phenomenon: the growing force of home-based entrepreneurs.

❝ *There are more than 2.1 million home-based businesses in the UK...(with) a combined turnover of over £364 billion in 2007. Over 60% of new businesses are started at home...approximately 1,400 new businesses each week, and the highest growth area is that of mothers, young people and the over-50s.* ❞
  Work-life balance, survey of members, Federation of Small Businesses, 2008[12]

Forget the 'pin money' myth!

There is a common assumption that home-based businesses (HBBs) are run by mums for pocket money. Partly for this reason there is little policy or support devoted to them. These are the hidden entrepreneurs. This is aggravated by the lack of registration by many HBBs because people are concerned they will have to pay business rates or their mortgage might be affected.

But let's put paid to the myths. Women do not outnumber men working from home; and some HBBs are substantial:

❝ *Just 14% of HBBs are wholly owned by women;*
26% of HBBs have an annual turnover of £100,000 or more. ❞
  Report, Hunter Centre for Entrepreneurship,
  the University of Strathclyde, 2009[13]

HBB turnovers are generally smaller than those of non-home-based small businesses (i.e., in commercial premises), but people are earning a decent income. Again, from the Hunter Centre study, it is reported that a quarter of HBBs earn between £26,000 and £50,000.

Professor Sara Carter, of the Hunter Centre for Entrepreneurship, and joint author of the above research, points out that HBBs generally have lower overheads, so turnover is close to income. She says, 'In comparison with average earnings (around £23,000), perhaps self-employment does fairly well.'

❛ *Views of home-based businesses have polarised around two stereotypes. One view dismisses home-based businesses as comprising lifestyle or hobby businesses, largely run by women to fit around childcare and household responsibilities and generating low incomes, and therefore economically insignificant. This view encourages government at all levels to ignore home-based businesses in their economic development strategies. The alternative perspective highlights the economic, social and environmental benefits of home-based business – strengthening local economies through job creation and commercial linkages, thereby reducing local economic leakages, enlivening daytime neighbourhoods (in both rural areas and suburban dormitory suburbs) thereby increasing their safety and security, and benefiting the environment.* ❜

Hunter Centre for Entrepreneurship, the University of Strathclyde, 2009[14]

So while not in the majority, nor working for 'pin money', women working from home are very much a part of this social revolution. And they are helped by the developments in IT over the past generation, enabling distance selling, 'outside office hours' working and global communications from the desktop.

Does your business fit?

Home for the change of life entrepreneurs needs to be adapted as the business often requires more than a computer and a telephone. Sometimes your home is your business, as with bed and breakfast, holiday accommodation or child-minding. Storage for the direct sellers can be an issue as boxes of books, cards or smellies need more than a cupboard. Coaches and counsellors must have a private room (or big enough garden office) and keep records secure. And no matter how big a kitchen table you have, it's not very practical to be clearing everything away each day.

❛ *I wanted my company to work around my children's school hours and so I have a home office. This was originally in a (converted) cupboard under the stairs in my kitchen! I've recently moved house so I am soon going to have the luxury of a room to myself to work in. I can't wait!* ❜

Tabitha Harman, Mimimyne

The home can make a practical working base, but you must take it seriously and give your business the space and privacy it needs in a household.

Also, as mentioned before, you may need to register your business at your home if you have a dedicated, or modified, space. This could make you liable for business rates so check with your local authority. And you will need appropriate insurance as work accidents or thefts cannot be claimed on household policies. Check this with your insurer or broker. The same goes for any vehicles you use for business.

‘ *My stress levels weren't eased when my neighbour reported me to the Council for running the classes from home. Fortunately, I had already informed them and they were happy with what I was doing.* ’

Charlotte Carr, Kiddy Cook franchisee

The FSB survey found that home-based entrepreneurs mostly wanted to grow their business, but not necessarily by employing people. Outsourcing was a popular tool. It also showed that women, more than men, 'value the ability to accommodate family needs'.

‘ *The flipside of the positive experiences . . .difficulties can often arise with things such as space, parking, IT and . . .the lack of any real boundaries between work and leisure, and the encroachment of work into "family time".* ’

Work-life balance, survey of members, Federation of Small Businesses, 2008[15]

Re-evaluate in mid-career

CASE STUDY

The Chocolate Tailor, founded by Jackie Roberts
www.chocolatetailor.co.uk
Business: manufacture of handmade chocolates, truffles and moulded figures, all freshly made in small quantities, using Belgian couverture chocolate and simple (real) ingredients.

Jackie Roberts set up her business, at home, in October 2005 after cannily practising for a few months while still working. She was a lecturer teaching business studies, in particular setting up in business, so she was about to follow her own teachings. Or was she?

'I had reached a "crossroads". Bereavement and a "Reflection" unit on a staff development course made me re-evaluate my position; I decided I didn't want to stay in education until I drew my pension.

There was no long-held dream, no sudden epiphany. I just thought no-one would employ a broken-down old lecturer, so I had to find something which might earn me enough to keep my house and a car (at the time, a Jaguar!) running. I didn't have any bankable skills or hobbies but I did have a long-term relationship with chocolate (eating it mainly). I took myself to Manchester on a half-day recreational course where I learned the easy way to temper chocolate. I gave some items I made to my friends and colleagues, who were impressed, so I thought that maybe I could do this as a business.'

What is her proposition?

'I believed there was a niche for this type of luxury product, and this has proved to be true, even through the recession. My ethos is to produce small batches of chocolates by hand either as a bespoke order, or for direct personal sales.

The chocolates are sold in presentation boxes for wedding and party favours, and corporate gifts. However, most of my sales are at farmers' and specialist food markets, and special public and private seasonal events. The majority of my clients are women.

The product is unique, as it is locally made and fresh: although chocolate can be stored for several months without any problem, my customers are eating it within days of its production.'

How did she prepare for her business?

'Despite having taught "Setting up Your Own Business", I didn't do any specific market research other than confirm that there was no one else in my area who was offering this type of service and product. However, I am careful to research any new steps or suppliers, usually via the internet.

Nor did I do a business plan – contrary to my own teaching! I didn't need finance and had I produced a written business plan, the reality would have deviated greatly. During my first year, particularly, I encountered many new contacts and new opportunities which I had never considered.

I did have an appointment with a Business Link adviser, but I didn't find this particularly useful. Perhaps it was because I was further down the line. My training was important though. After the initial chocolate course at Slattery's in Manchester, I enrolled on a more intensive 2-day course to ensure that I did enjoy working with chocolate and to develop my skills enough to start a business.'

So how is the business doing?
'I operate as a sole trader, working from home. In general, the plan "in my head" did work and is still working. I have always been in profit and although I live on a much lower income than before, I still have a good standard of living. I am much happier and more fulfilled.

As a single woman, I can work when I like without having to consider family commitments. Therefore I can start work at 5 am if I want, and I can have time off when I want (or am forced to down tools if there is a heatwave). However, peak times at Christmas mean I am working 7 days a week, often for 14 hours a day which is physically demanding. Then I ask friends to help me with presentation and packing.'

What difficulties has she encountered?
'The only time I have experienced a doubt of confidence was when trying to get to grips with the rules and regulations of Trading Standards' labelling, weighing and packaging. Wading though instructions which seem so incomprehensible and irrelevant to an artisan chocolatier! However, I think I have cracked it now. The frustration came from wanting to get everything right.

Also, I do wish I hadn't believed everyone I met who would take my time and my samples and say they would be in touch with an order. Now I am more sceptical, and I choose who I do business with. I still dislike poor business etiquette.

I would like to develop my chocolatier techniques further but the only government scheme I have come across is "Train To Gain", which is for employees, not proprietors.'

CHAPTER TWENTY FIVE

THE RISE OF THE MUMPRENEUR

❝ The best advice and contacts I have made have been through a forum called Mumsclub (www.mumsclub.co.uk), set up by Jane Hopkins. It is a fantastic group of women all running their own businesses and we support each other, give advice and share the problems of trying to be a mumpreneur! ❞

Cari Parker, The Dales Party Company

Join the supermums

I haven't found the origins of this rather cringe-making word but if you put 'mumpreneur' into a search engine, you will find a world of supermums. They are running businesses, networking, finding part-time jobs for other mums and forming a host of online shops (mostly selling baby stuff). Many of them network, both online and face to face; there are groups to join and awards to be won. You will find many of these listed in the Appendix.

In some ways, new mothers have an advantage when it comes to starting a business.

■ Firstly, they are not in work (or decide not to go back) so there is no well-paid job holding them back.

■ There is often (not always) a main income via their partner, so this reduces the financial pressure on the new business.

And there is an underlying purpose: many mums start a business to provide the stimulation of their former careers (although working from home doesn't always provide social contact). Networking has really come into its own for this entrepreneurial group.

❝ I've found lots of my fellow entrepreneurs on Twitter and other social networks have been very helpful with advice and ideas, and to give

something back, I've started a series of regular "Mumpreneur" meetups (which are sponsored by BTTradespace) and feature speakers who have learned everything they know by doing it themselves. 〉

Tabitha Harman, Mimimyne info@mimimyne.com

Karen Sherr's top tips for mumpreneurs

- Research the market and competition.
- Start small, let the business grow as and when you can cope with expansion.
- Have a clear idea what you want out of the business.
- Try to separate work from home. If your business is based at home, have a second phoneline fitted.
- Have backup. If your child is ill, what will happen to your business?
- Know your limitations. For example, if you have problems with accounts, get someone to help you.
- If there are not enough hours in the day to do everything, do the bits you like (with both work and home life) and get help with the bits you don't.
- Work out the balance between work and home that you want.
- Keep time to be a mum.
- Set time aside to deal with administration, household tasks etc. If you keep putting it off, the task will become huge (hours of paperwork, for example, or loads of ironing) – regular manageable chunks of mundane but important tasks will help things flow smoothly.

(Karen Sherr of Musical Minis)

Get through post-natal depression

CASE STUDY

The Dales Party Company, incorporating Party Sprite and Coochie Cou, founded by Cari Parker
www.partysprite.co.uk and www.coochiecou.co.uk
Business: Party Sprite sells party supplies and does event decoration, and Coochie Cou organises family events. They trade with consumers at the moment but have plans to wholesale and do corporate events.

Cari is something of a serial mumpreneur. She left her job in 2004 taking on direct selling jobs and is still an agent for Usborne Books. She started Party Sprite in January 2008, formed The Dales Party Company in June and then started working on Coochie Cou. She had set up a business in her early 20s that did not take off so she brought hard experience to her ventures:

'I had always wanted to be self employed. I found working for an employer stifled my creativity and I often felt I had a better way of doing things. I didn't really research my first product very well and the sales did not come, so reluctantly I went back to work. I fell into retail and learnt a lot about cash handling, stock and dealing with customers. After two children I knew I needed to try something that was just mine. I did some research and when a friend decided to sell her party supplies business, I agreed to buy it. My eldest was approaching school age and was going to parties, which put me in contact with my target market. I have always loved children's parties, organising them for my younger sister when we were children.

Coochie Cou came into being from a conversation; we had plans to start corporate events but to fit in with our family theme it quickly evolved into baby fairs and mothers' markets in North Yorkshire and Teeside.'

How did she view the risk?
'I knew from the start that it was a big risk. We don't have a lot of money to spare as my husband is on low pay, and we were unable to borrow from the banks. So everything has had to be done to a strict budget and I have had to do a lot myself, such as setting up the websites. I also needed the flexibility of working around my children, when they were asleep or playing together. Things are easier now they are both in childcare and my youngest will soon be starting school so I can do all my work during the day.'

What planning did she do?
'I have done business plans in the past but have yet to do one for now. It is on my "to do" list as I have recently bought Antonia Chitty's book and it has inspired me to get my finger out and set out my aims and objectives on paper.'

How did she balance work and family needs?
'With huge conflict! Running a family home with two children to look after and then try and throw working into the mix is enough to drive the sanest person mad. But the focus is on providing a better life for my children and for that to happen, I need to be working. We don't have

any relatives close enough to help out with childcare so I have had to work quite a few late nights to get the business off the ground. My aim from the start was to combine working with being there for the children and watching them grow up, so the work had to fit around the children and not the other way.

I knew that it wouldn't be easy but I have amazing support from my husband and while the house isn't spotless, my girls are fed, clothed and loved and will hopefully have some lovely memories of mummy being around for them. I have seen my parents raise my sister's children as she works full time and it made me determined to be there for all the milestones with my own children.'

It hasn't been without struggles

'I have battled with post-natal depression (PND) following both births. I still have a fear of using the phone which makes work extremely difficult, but I am fighting and have found a confidence I never knew I had. Pushing yourself into the public eye is hard when you have low confidence and poor self image, but I have a lot of fight and a lot of support.

After PND, cash flow has to be the greatest challenge. We don't have any spare cash to bail out the business, meaning I have to be so strict with expenditure and make sure we don't hang on to any stock.

And my husband has been unemployed twice since I started, which has put a lot of strain on everything. While he did help with watching the children I found he got under my feet a lot. It is certainly easier with him at work.'

Is there anything she wishes she hadn't done?

'In the early days I paid a professional designer to do some work for me and I now realise the business was not able to justify such a huge expense. If I had shopped around I could have had the work done to as high a standard but at a fraction of the cost.'

What is a real positive?

'I believe networking is very important and I am actively involved in online social media networking as well as through my events. While any networking is useful, I find that the women's groups, and in particular other mums, meet my needs the most. They truly understand the trials and tribulations we have every day.'

CHAPTER TWENTY SIX

SEEK OUT THE RIGHT HELP FOR YOU

Overcome a disadvantage

People in difficult circumstances don't fit the image of the successful entrepreneur. But with the right help they can work for themselves and develop a going concern. If you are unemployed, homeless or an ex-offender, there is help around. Information is available from Business Link, your local Job Centre or the organisations mentioned here. Further details are in the Appendix. All these schemes are live at the time of writing; obviously these can change.

If you have been successful and would like to support women in disadvantaged situations, visit the websites and see how welcome your help would be.

Homeless
Crisis helps homeless people become self employed through Crisis Changing Lives.

Unemployed
InBiz is a company helping unemployed people into self employment and business creation. It works with organisations such as Jobcentre Plus, Business Link[16] and the Learning and Development Councils.

Tackle mental illness and unemployment

CASE STUDY
Pauline Robson, co-owner of Meze
Business: Turkish restaurant in Darlington, County Durham

Pauline really has overcome adversity to set up her business. She has suffered mental illness and homelessness following a divorce and bereavement. She was close to a breakdown and was living on incapacity benefit. She recounts her experience without any self-pity:

'Despite what had happened, I wanted to get back to work. But it's not easy to get back into the workplace after mental illness. There is discrimination and I hadn't worked for 12 years, so I knew I had to work for myself. If anything, this spurred me on.'

How did she get started?
'It took two years to open. I had a friend, a Turkish chef called Cem Eskiki, who ran a pizza restaurant. He was opening a Turkish restaurant and I helped him get the place ready. His partner then dropped out and I wanted to buy in. I came across InBiz, but found out I could only get half the finance I needed; I had to provide the other half. I didn't have two pennies to rub together and I was on £83 a week incapacity benefit, so I couldn't do it. Cem found another partner.

I didn't give up, though. I found another property and Cem helped me with this. Then InBiz contacted me and put me on to the Pinetrees Trust and they were prepared to give me a £3,000 loan from their Spirit of Enterprise Loan Fund. This was on the basis that Cem came in with me, which he did. I also got some help from the Shaw Trust and Global Grants. So we were off.'

How was the process for her?
'I had to sign a piece of paper saying I wouldn't go off the rails again, which I found really annoying. How do I know what could happen? But I signed it.

The support ends after a year and it hasn't been easy. I am grateful for the help I got from Annette Semple (adviser at In Biz), but some ongoing mentoring would be really useful right now. We've been through a long recession and a severe winter when no one came out to eat for over a month. There's no safety net; you're on your own.'

So what is business like now?
'We don't get a wage, but the business is ticking over. We seat 18 people, five days a week and it's just Cem and myself. We're alright, we're managing. To stay open in a recession, when bigger restaurants are closing, is an achievement.'

What advice does she offer to others in her situation?
'If you have mental illness, you need to search out the help. You can do it, it's all about feeling good about yourself; but you need a helping hand.'

Ex-offenders

Startup offers ex-offenders and those about to be released from prison the opportunity to become self-employed. It works with both men and women, although the focus for 2010 is the Startupnow for Women project as a response to the Corston Report.[17]

> ❛ Self-employment suits women coming out of prison at so many levels. They've often built up impressive lists of qualifications and training in prison but come out with no funding or support to become self-employed. We have found that with relatively little funding but loads of basic business advice and a personal mentor, these women have flourished, with their self esteem rocketing.
>
> Not only have they thrived on becoming financially independent but it's obviously positive for their families and the community as a whole. Over the last three years we have seen under five per cent re-offending rate from Startup supported clients and, in fact, have had no women who have returned to prison once they have set up their own business. Our Startupnow for Women project offers advice on self-employment and personal development to 240 women, with 60 going on to set up their own business. ❜
>
> Juliet Hope, Chief Executive, Startup

New kids on the block

> ❛ Generation Y, the "digital generation", is predicted to be highly entrepreneurial and their digital technology focus means that many of their businesses are likely to be home-based. Rising costs of commuting, the increase in congestion and the introduction of carbon taxes will encourage more and more people to work from home. ❜
>
> Hunter Centre for Entrepreneurship, the University of Strathclyde, 2009[18]

Every recession hits the young hard. The job market dries up for trainees and graduate recruitment schemes shrink. Many young people are being encouraged to become self-employed, despite the lack of work experience.

> ❛ The Prince's Trust helps disadvantaged young people in the UK not in employment, education or training. It has helped more than 600,000 young people since 1976 and supports over 100 more each working day. More than three in four young people The Trust helped last year moved into work, education or training.

■ *It has helped more than 74,000 young people set up in business since 1983.*

■ *56% of Trust-supported businesses are trading into their third year.*

■ *The Trust needs to raise almost £1 million every week to continue our vital work.* ❯

The Prince's Trust

Adapt and bounce back

Case Study
Love Food Festival, created and run by Lorna Knapman
www.lovefoodfestival.com
Business: Food festivals based in the SouthWest of England

Lorna Knapman's enthusiasm and love of life comes across in spades (just see her website!) This translates into the food festivals she creates, where people can buy local food from small producers and traders in the West Country. Her target turnover for 2009/10 was £35,000. However, her venture was borne out of adverse conditions: Lorna was ill in her teens and did not get the exam results she was capable of. She became unemployed and had a breakdown. She takes up her story at the age of 28:

'I went to the Prince's Trust with the idea of setting up a juice bar. It was a good idea, but then I discovered I was pregnant. I was on my own and after Ned was born, I found life as a new mum pretty tricky; the first few months were really difficult. But the Prince's Trust kept in touch, in the background, supporting me. When Ned was eight months old, I got a new mentor, Erica Thomas, and we went through lots of ideas together.

My first venture was Bite Size, healthy food for children at festivals. I was interested in food and nutrition, and through weaning Ned I got interested in children's nutrition.'

Why didn't it work?
'I was appointed the children's food caterer for the Soil Association. I was so excited, I thought this was a real breakthrough, but it turned out to be a complete disaster. All the big companies at these festivals gave away free food to kids so my food didn't sell. It put me out of business

and I lost the money I invested in it. However, it gave me a better idea.'

The big idea
'Instead of catering at existing events I decided to set up my own food festival, one that would really educate people and have plenty of food-related activities for children. People could come for free and buy good, local food from market stalls. I ran the first one in May 2009; I expected around 400 people and over a thousand turned up! I've not looked back since then.'

Was self employment always on the cards?
'Yes. I've always wanted to work for myself. I was rebellious and went off the rails as a teenager, so I've always wanted to develop my ideas and express myself. Then when I had Ned, I got work as a waitress and the hours were awful. My mum helped to look after him but I was finishing shifts at midnight, it was impossible. However, there was another light bulb moment. I worked at the Paintworks in Bristol and realised what a great venue it was, so that firmed up my ideas.'

What help does she get?
'I have two freelancers working with me now who are brilliant. There are people who do the design and photography. And my greatest help is Erica. She is a steady support; she doesn't tell me what to do but she really listens to me and encourages me. It's difficult out there on your own; you need a sanity-check every so often. She is amazing. I want to make her proud of me.'

Life has taken off!
'I won the Prince's Trust SouthWest Enterprise Award and I've recently become an ambassador for them. I lecture to groups of young people and I went to Downing Street and met the Prime Minister for a reception to celebrate community heroes.'

And the future?
'I hope that my festivals will help people realise that eating healthily can be easy and fun. My events include children zones, cooking workshops, circus performers, herb gardens...you name it. I encourage local business start-ups to take stalls which will help them grow. I've built up a strong brand and my next event will see around 4,000 people attend over two days. There'll be more than 80 stalls, a demo kitchen, healing area, library section, cinema – it's the biggest event I'll hold to date.

I don't make a huge amount of money at the moment, I get by. But the business is growing and that's the reward. The brand is strong now and we are taking the festival on tour around the country. I'm working with some really great people and the future looks very bright!

Life is so different now. There were times when I couldn't get out of the house, and now I have so much confidence. I'm really enjoying things, I love the business. And Ned is so confident too; it was a difficult start for us but this has helped us get through it.'

❛ *The National Council for Graduate Entrepreneurship began in 2004 with the aim of fostering a culture of entrepreneurship throughout the higher education sector. One of its key targets is to increase the numbers of students and graduates considering self employment or starting a business. Through its programme* Flying Start *it offers support and helps with funding from grants, public funds and business angels for former and leaving students keen to set up in business.* ❜

National Council for Graduate Entrepreneurship (NCGE)

Ian Robertson, NCGE Chief Executive, says young people are quite ready to go into business: 'What is the point of spending a few years in a menial job, even in a good company, when you could be getting things done on your own? Technology has brought the future forward; you can set up a global business from your desktop. There is a lot of support today.'

So the days of the entrepreneur setting up after 20 years' technical and market experience in a multinational are dwindling.

❛ *Over the next five years, big companies are not going to be employing large numbers of people like they have in the past. They are outsourcing a lot of their requirements. So self employment becomes an absolute career option.* ❜

Ian Robertson, Chief Executive, NCGE

The grey revolution

Older people are working for themselves in increasing numbers, often from home. This reflects our improving health and longevity, and quite possibly the pressure on our pensions. There is no specific organisation championing this sector of self employment, but welcome women of all ages as do the women's business groups.

❛ . . . it seems inevitable that the home will become even more important as a focus for business activity in the future. Demographic trends will be a key driver. The ageing of the population, increasing longevity and improved health means that there will be more and more people of post-retirement age who either wish to continue to be economically active or have a financial imperative to do so. Thus, we can expect to see more older people running businesses from home in semi-retirement. ❜

Hunter Centre for Entrepreneurship, the University of Strathclyde, 2009[19]

The disabled entrepreneur

❛ People with a disability are often put off by the traditional language of business. . . (they) are often likely to see starting a business as a route to work which complements their values or enables them to balance their lives, rather than an end in itself. ❜

Enabled4Enterprise, Leonard Cheshire Disability, 2009[20]

More inclusion please

The above report highlights that disabled people are not only, in many cases, excluded from the workplace, but they do not easily access the mainstream business support organisations. So it is important for those organisations to understand the wide range of disability and empathise with disabled clients. See the Appendix for support.

❛ 3% of respondents were disabled.

16.5% of those started their business because they had difficulty finding paid employment (compared to 10% for those with no disability). However, they were happier with their work than able-bodied respondents. ❜

Work-life balance, survey of members, Federation of Small Businesses, 2008[21]

Match your ability to the market

Case Study

Four Paws Aqua, established and run by Karen Standen
www.fourpawsaqua.co.uk
Business: canine hydrotherapy for injured or sick dogs

Karen Standen has had many challenges getting her venture afloat (literally).

She set up in business because she had difficulty keeping a regular office job due to her dyslexia. She has worked in factory jobs, as a care worker and began training as a social worker. Now Karen has found her calling:

'When you tell people you have dyslexia they think you can't read or write. I definitely experienced discrimination when I applied for jobs. I got the idea for Four Paws Aqua when my Labrador, Chum, broke his leg twice. The vet recommended hydrotherapy for him but the nearest pool was 25 miles away with a six month waiting list. So in 2007 I did some research and decided there was a demand for this service locally.

My mum helped me leaflet vets' surgeries and postcards in shop windows and soon people were phoning asking when I would be opening! I started with 47 customers and now I have 400 from a 40 mile radius. The dogs love to get into the water; it's warm and it eases pain, stiffness and swelling.

I work from a business centre with my own therapy pool, which my husband built. It is a specialised pool with a ramp and a hoist that can lift 30 stone, for dogs with impaired mobility. We follow a strict hygiene regime.

We recently moved to a bigger unit at the front of the building so now people can get access after office hours.'

What help did she get as a disabled person?
'I had to be pro-active and find out about things myself – you've got to fight for things. But I did get lots of local support: from Business Link, training and support group Women's Wisdom and I went on a course run by disability charity ENHAM. They provided me with a great mentor, John Fox, who helped me with my business plan. I also received training and computer equipment from Ready to Start, which was run by Leonard Cheshire Disability.

I don't have a good credit rating so the banks wouldn't lend to me. I nearly lost my home at one point, but I became a woman obsessed with the idea. I got £350 from ENHAM for marketing materials and a £5,000 loan from charity Frederick's Foundation. That paid for my pool.'

Does she cope with the business side of things?
'I don't like writing emails. If I can't read something my husband or my

PA read it to me. She writes my letters. And I confess I'm not very good at cash flow, which is why we nearly lost our home. ENHAM helped again here and I have some software for that now. I'm learning to run my website myself, that saves a lot of money.'

Not content with just running a business...
'I set up a women's networking group for Portsmouth. I couldn't be doing with getting up at 6 am and sitting around with a load of boring men. They look at you as if you are a piece of dirt, so I now run the group from my business unit. It's 50p a meeting and we are great support for each other.

And the business has diversified into other dog services such as physiotherapy, grooming and walking. We are also running a dog show in Portsmouth in summer.'

And how is her business developing?
'I have had ups and downs. It's been a real challenge. Now I have competition setting up, one of my ex-customers. But he's not going to beat me.

As I employ volunteers, I am learning how to become a social enterprise. That feels like the right way to go.'

CHAPTER TWENTY SEVEN

VENTURES WITH A DIFFERENCE

The franchising option

❝ *27% of all franchisees are female. This has continued to grow, with 34% of recruits over the last two years being female.* ❞

The British Franchise Association (BFA)

Many people choose to expand their business by offering their 'model' for someone to run within a specified geographic region. Some of these franchises are big names with purchase costs to match. More recently though, some successful family-friendly enterprises have begun to expand this way (see the Case Studies in Chapter 28).

❝ *The term "franchising" has been used to describe many different forms of business relationships, including licensing, distributor and agency arrangements. The more popular use of the term has arisen from the development of what is called "business format franchising". (This) is the granting of permission by one person (the franchisor) to another (the franchisee), entitling the franchisee to trade under the trade mark/trade name of the franchisor.* ❞

The British Franchise Association website[22]

Some household names that are franchises:
- Bang & Olufsen
- Clark's Shoes
- Dominos Pizza
- Kall Kwik
- McDonald's
- Pitman Training
- Stagecoach Theatre Arts
- Thorntons
- Toni and Guy
- Tumble Tots
- Wimpy

TRY THIS

Think about whether franchising would suit you?

Pros	Cons
You have a tried-and-tested business proposition.	Franchises can be very expensive to buy and it doesn't guarantee you success.
You are buying a package, so as an untrained person, you can gain the necessary skills and information from one source to start your business.	You don't have the satisfaction of originating an idea and seeing it flourish.
You receive ongoing support: training, product development, advertising, promotional activities and with a specialist range of management services.	You have to pay ongoing management service fees.
You are the owner and operator of the franchised business; you have autonomy and its success is down to your effort and talent.	The franchisor retains control over the way in which products and services are marketed and sold, and controls the quality and standards of the business.
If you choose a good franchise, you should be buying an asset which can grow in value. It is saleable and transferable (within the terms of the franchise agreement) and if you are successful, it should increase in value.	The value, and your capital gain, is limited to your geographic area. You won't make the money that the franchisor does!

What does it cost?

The lower end of the market is around the £5,000 mark, which will usually consist of a home-based style operation. The costs start to increase as you bring in specialist machinery, vehicles, premises etc.

Do your homework

It goes without saying, the kind of business you can run is limited by what is available (and your 'patch' may already be taken). And you need to be flexible as it is unlikely you will find a business that is run exactly how you would set it up. While relevant experience is not always required, it obviously helps that you have a background in the field of your chosen franchise. An interest in . . . printing, cleaning, children's play, retail . . . is a must.

Do your homework on the franchisor too. If it is a BFA member, they have some credentials as all members have to conform to its standards, Code of Ethics and disciplinary procedures. It could also influence your credit appeal.

Tom Endean, marketing manager at the BFA, says, 'A BFA member franchise is a better proposition than most business start-ups with regards to risk, so banks that understand franchising are more likely to help with finance. HSBC, Lloyds TSB and RBS/NatWest have BFA recognised specialist departments. These are better people to talk to if you want to look at finance.'

Ask if the franchisor has done any market or competitor research in your area. Also, talk to some of their existing franchisees. The BFA has a guide on becoming a franchisee and runs seminars too.[23]

Meet the challenge of a franchise

CASE STUDY
Kiddy Cook franchise, owned and run by Charlotte Carr
(see franchisor Nikki Geddes Case Study in Chapter 28)
www.kiddycook.co.uk
Business: Running cookery classes and parties for children 2–11 years old

Charlotte became the first franchisee of Kiddy Cook in May 2009, based in Leighton Buzzard. She currently works alone and runs the classes from her home or at local village halls in her area. Originally she was going to stay at home with her son until he was of school age, but her plans changed when he was two.

'I was a retailer for 23 years before having my son. After a couple of years two realities hit home. Firstly my husband's income alone didn't leave us much to enjoy life with, and secondly, I became a little depressed about being at home on my own every day.

I have always found it hard to sit still for long so I started looking for opportunities. A full time job wasn't suitable and I didn't want to work for someone else under their terms. I wanted to share my energies between my family and working, so that my brain didn't turn completely to mush!'

How did she feel about taking on a franchise?
'I was scared stiff! Having been employed my whole life, the thought of total success or failure resting on me was very scary. Two years "out" can knock your confidence. However, it was also a buzz. And being a franchise, the hard work and mistakes had already been made. I felt I could benefit from Nikki's experience and be successful more quickly.

There wasn't the chance to procrastinate as the franchise was being offered at a much lower cost for a short period of time. This meant taking a quick decision, and after some legal advice I took advantage of the offer.'

How did you research the potential?
'I talked to lots of people about what they thought of the concept and everyone I spoke to was positive. I also checked out what other classes were available in the area and found that there was a gap in the market.

In terms of planning, I looked at how I could make the money I wanted and how many hours this would take, on a monthly basis. I did this both on my own and with the franchisor.'

Is there any conflict between work and family demands?
'At the moment I am probably doing more hours than I originally wanted, but as I get more organised it is getting easier. I have the work/ life balance that suits me – that was one of the key drivers in my decision.'

What has helped you the most?
'Talking to friends, family and franchisor helped enormously but Nikki has been my best adviser. I couldn't have done it without her support.

Also, I have developed a friendship with a woman who set up a music class in the area a few weeks before me. We exchange ideas and experiences and that has been invaluable. I hope to start networking soon when I get more childcare in place. Just knowing that someone is going through the same process as me is hugely reassuring.'

And what was your greatest challenge?
'The biggest challenge was getting people through the door! I am building up my marketing and numbers slowly, which suits me. The more confident I become, the more children I can handle in the class.

Another obstacle I had was finding someone to insure me to do the classes at home. That is two days of my life I will never get back!'

And how is business doing?
'I have finished my first term and have two classes, a contract with the local SureStart centre and a hugely oversubscribed after-school club. Not bad for a new business in a recession!

I would recommend that anyone who is not quite ready to start completely from scratch to go for the franchise option – providing you choose carefully. Not all afford as much freedom to be creative as mine does.'

The direct selling route

‘ *Last year, over 300,000 people started their own independent business working with a direct selling company – up 11% on the previous year – and 88% were women. Most did so because they wanted a separate source of part time income.*

The majority of direct sellers spend a few hours a week and earn under £1,000 a year. However, for the 30,000 plus full time women and men, incomes in excess of £50,000 pa are not exceptional. ’

Direct Selling Association

Direct selling and network marketing are methods of selling goods directly to the consumer. They are the UK's largest provider of part time earnings, responsible for turning school fairs into tempting market places and homes into lingerie parlours!

Income comes from two sources: selling the product, at a profit; and building a team and earning from their sales.

The sale is usually made face to face:

■ a product is demonstrated in the home, often at a party or coffee morning
■ a catalogue is left with the customer
■ a product is sold at local markets and fairs.

❝ *I've been a full-time mum looking after my children for five years and I wanted to do something for myself. It was minimal set-up cost so I just said to myself that I would try it, and if it didn't work out, that was fine. I am based at home and go to people's houses, playgroups and fairs. I haven't needed to do any complex financial planning. So far it has fitted in well with my home life and my sales are building up.* ❞

Alex Glover, Usborne Books distributor

Richard Berry, director of the Direct Selling Association (DSA), explains its appeal: 'A high proportion of new business start-ups fail and the main reason is that the business concept is untried and proves to be unprofitable. This is why franchising is popular as it is a proven business format. However, taking up a franchise is unaffordable for many women, who do not have substantial savings. The great strength of a direct selling business opportunity is that it is tried and proven to work.'

Advantages of becoming a direct selling distributor (DSD):

■ It offers total flexibility in terms of time and effort.
■ It is universally affordable – the average cost of taking up a business opportunity with a DSA member company is under £100.
■ It offers complete independence.

Richard Berry adds, 'Like running any business, it is not an easy source of income. But if a woman takes the advice that is offered, learns from others in the same direct selling company and perseveres, then it can be hugely rewarding. Today, around the world, over 90 million women are benefiting from the opportunities provided by direct selling companies.'

Some examples of popular direct selling brands:

■ Avon Cosmetics
■ Betterware UK
■ Kleeneze
■ Phoenix Trading (see below)
■ The Body Shop at Home
■ The Pampered Chef
■ Usborne Books at Home

Membership of the DSA gives a brand credibility, but you should still do your research.

TRY THIS

Ask tough questions before you sign up (and add more of your own)

▶ How does it work and how do I make my money?

▶ Can you give me an indication as to how much money I might make?

▶ How much product do I have to store at home?

▶ What do I have to pay you (now and in the future?)

▶ Can I give up if I don't like it?

▶ Can I talk to another vendor (not the person 'signing you up')?

▶ Will I get any money back if I can't sell?

Build a team and earn bonuses

CASE STUDY
Phoenix Trading: co-founder, Robin Bradley www.phoenix-trading.co.uk
Business: a global, independent card-publishing house with 12,000 traders and 78 artists

You may well know a Phoenix trader in your local community. The business was started, classically, in 1995 by three mothers at the kitchen table, with £30 investment. It grew slowly and organically, offering (almost exclusively) women an unpressurised business opportunity that they could all do in exactly the same way. It is now one of the top ten greeting card publishers in the UK. One of the founding three, Robin Bradley, is still at the helm:

'Essentially, we have recruited in our own image. Most women who join us want a low key, supportive environment and many of them are traders for social, rather than commercial, reasons. This is not typical in an industry which tends to be very target orientated.

Although we are not the most dynamic direct selling business in the country we have still managed to build a team of traders turning over £12m plus a year. The most successful trader earns a not insignificant £250,000 a year in bonuses.'

CASE STUDY
Phoenix Trading, independent trader Sue May
Business: network marketing based on retailing greetings cards and other stationery products from home.

Robin describes Sue as 'efficient, focused, organised, late 40s and articulate'. She has been a part time trader since 2000 and has a total team of over 1,300 in France, US, Australia and New Zealand and the UK. She has a background in selling and had been involved with a network marketing company, selling books, prior to joining Phoenix. She sells in her local community but is also an Executive Trader (ET) with a team of agents to support. She earns over £60,000 in bonuses and profit:

'The need to earn was secondary to my overwhelming desire to do something other than look after babies and talk about babies with other mums. I wanted to do something that I was in control of, involving other people. I had worked for years in corporate environments and decided I much preferred the freedom to be my own boss.

The previous network marketing company had stopped unexpectedly owing to a takeover. I had parties already booked for the Christmas season and I had joined another book selling company. I came across Phoenix cards, so I thought I would do both books and cards. I kept separate accounts and decided to see which one worked, and which one I enjoyed. The book selling company went under and Phoenix was a joy to be involved with. Deliveries turned up on time and were accurate and it was great being involved with such a friendly company.'

So how does it work?
'Some traders just sell cards, but we are encouraged to recruit other traders, known as sponsoring. I receive a 5% bonus from Phoenix based on my sponsees' monthly performance, provided that I achieve a certain amount of monthly volume myself (perfectly achievable). This means I can't sit back and do nothing while all the people I've signed up work.

I became an ET by sponsoring five people and building to a certain volume for two months in a row. This is when you can really start to make a difference to your income, as you get 5% of all your downline volume (people your sponsees have recruited), not just those you have sponsored.

Some sponsees need a lot of support and others don't want any input. I have personally sponsored 75 people in the UK, one in New Zealand and one in the US. Out of those 77, some have gone on to become ETs themselves and built up their own teams, some have stopped and some just carry on at a pace that suits them. The more people I can sponsor, the better, as you never know who will turn out to be very good. I feel obliged to support my team as I earn through them, and motivated because I want to earn more.

Arguably I could do a lot less and still earn the same amount from Phoenix but this would only last for the short term. People would lose interest if they weren't being looked after properly. It is also rewarding getting to know people better and seeing them achieve what they want.'

How has her business grown?
'My business has grown enormously. For the first few years it doubled; now it has slowed down, reflecting the growth in the economy. But it is by no means static, and you have to keep growing in order to continue.'

What does she put her success down to?
'I think my success is due to my confidence and enthusiasm which transmit to other people. Also my honesty in explaining how things are. And a certain degree of luck in finding some other good people along the way, who have grown their businesses and thus mine too. I always go back to people quite quickly if they ask me anything. It is essential to keep people motivated and in touch.'

What is her advice to other women thinking about becoming an agent?
'Decide if it's a product you like. Ask yourself lots of questions. Can you build it in to your current lifestyle? Does the style of selling suit you? Do you have the time for daytime coffee mornings or can you do it alongside an existing job? What do you want from it? Does it involve demonstrations of any kind? Would you like that? What is the support from the company? What is the pressure from the company or an upline? Do you like what you've heard?'

The social enterprise

‘ *Social enterprises are businesses driven by a social or environmental purpose. There are 62,000 of them in the UK, contributing over £24bn to the economy, employing approximately 800,000 people* (2005–2007 data from the Annual Survey of Small Business UK).

As with all businesses, they compete to deliver goods and services. The difference is that social purpose is at the very heart of what they do, and the profits they make are reinvested towards achieving that purpose. Well-known examples *of social enterprises include The Big Issue, Jamie Oliver's restaurant* Fifteen, *and the fair-trade chocolate company Divine Chocolate.* ❯

Social Enterprise Coalition website[24]

Generate an idea at the school gate

CASE STUDY
Women Like Us, co-founded by Karen Mattison
www.womenlikeus.org.uk
Business: social enterprise helping women back into the workplace through part-time jobs

> '*There are so many women with children who want to work, but not at the expense of family life. At* Women Like Us *we bring women confidently back into the workplace after taking a break to raise a family. And, at all stages of their working lives, we help women find part-time or flexible work that uses their skills and talents.*'

That's how the Women Like Us website introduces itself and it describes its mission perfectly. Karen Mattison began the venture with her friend Emma Stewart in 2005. Karen describes how they pieced together the concept, tested it and then took the leap:

'Emma and I met when we worked together in jobs at a mental health charity. After I had my second child, I wanted to move on but still work part time; but I couldn't find anything for my level of experience on that basis. So I went freelance, helping charities and government bodies with business development. Emma did the same when she had her child. The work built up and I passed some to her, then we had more and we developed an informal network of freelancers.'

How did the idea develop?
'Our work brought us into contact with lots of employers and we realised

that, contrary to popular opinion, many of them liked part time workers in certain roles. It made us think. We were also meeting mums at the school gate who had been working, often in quite senior roles, but they couldn't find a way to get back into work on the basis they needed. We began to tell people about these jobs on an informal basis, the way the freelance work had developed. We thought there could be a business here.'

What was the next step?
'I live in North London and Emma lives in South East London so we began to meet in a hotel in Victoria, with one pot of tea lasting for hours! We didn't give up our jobs immediately, but we put together a concept that brought the employers and the women at the school gates together: *Women Like Us* was born.

With a basic business plan, a logo and a website we got a grant of £25,000 to set up a Community Interest Company (the legal form of social enterprise) from the then Department of Trade and Industry. The business can become profitable and staff can earn commercial rates and even bonuses. What we can't do is sell the business on.

We started with a pilot of 30 women, and in one term, ten of them had gained permanent, part time employment. So we realised we had a potential business.

There is a lot of support for what we are doing. The head teacher at my son's school recognised the benefit of mothers working part time and she allows us to put leaflets in the children's book bags. We now have partnerships with 200 schools across London. Word-of-mouth also brings a lot of women to us. We get the jobs by direct mailing employers. There is an element of educating employers about the value of part time workers as well.'

Why did they set up as a social enterprise?
'We are not motivated solely by finance. Our social mission is to find work for women that fits their family lives and does not reduce their value in the workplace. We offer women career coaching to build their confidence so that they don't get any job, they get the right job. Too often women take jobs that are below their skill level just because they are flexible: they are effectively trading their skills in return for flexibility.'

How do they differ from a recruitment agency?
'Being out of the workplace, whether just for maternity leave or longer, can reduce your self confidence and self esteem. So we offer a package of guidance, workshops and career coaching. This is a journey back to work.

We differ from a traditional recruitment agency in that we specialise in part time and flexible roles. We help employers to design jobs and then provide a full recruitment service. Often small businesses use our services because they understand the business benefits of part time. They want a £40k-calibre person but only have £20k to spend.'

Where is the business now?
'We have two offices in London and employ over 50 staff. Our annual turnover is approx £1.5 million.

Women contact us from elsewhere in the country saying they would like our service in their area, so there is potential to grow much bigger. We are ambitious for the business and would like to expand outside London. Some have asked us if we would franchise the business but it is a complex business model made up of coaching, recruitment, outreach and management of government contracts so, for the moment, we have ruled this out.'

Combine community and enterprise

CASE STUDY
PJs Community Services, developed by Claudine Reid MBE
www.patreid.co.uk
Business: A social enterprise based in Croydon, South London, providing services for the local authority and other public institutions

Claudine began her career unaware that she was on the path to entrepreneurial greatness. She began at PJs on a work placement, married the director, Patrick Reid, and with him took the company on to become the kind of enterprise every city community should have. Now Director of Operations, Claudine is also a Social Enterprise Ambassador, a Business Champion nominated by the London Borough of Croydon and has advised the government on Ethnic Minority Business issues. Here she shows there is a different face to the concept of entrepreneurship:

'PJs was founded in 1992 with a Prince's Trust grant and Patrick's redundancy money, as a home shopping service for elderly, house-bound people. We developed other services in the fields of youth work, education, business and the arts and became a trusted partner for our clients. We work with marginalised sections of the community, helping unemployed people back into work and providing training and enterprise development, parenting and educational programmes.

Education and youth are now key areas and we work with young people who are having trouble settling into school. We have programmes to help students make the transition to senior school and to give them practical skills.

One young man came back two years after he had left. He had been very disruptive and so angry, he had thought of slashing my car tyres. Now he is at college and doing voluntary work. In fact he came back to say 'Sorry'. It takes time and care, but people can turn around.'

What was the turning point for PJs?
'In 2001 we had the opportunity to buy a 9,000 square feet derelict warehouse, which we converted – a huge job. This was financed from our reserves and a commercial mortgage: no grants. It enabled us to create new facilities and move into new areas of work. We have meeting rooms, recording studios and an Ofsted approved nursery.

We transferred the home shopping service to another company so we are not involved in that any more. As a result we have become more efficient and we employ 35 people.'

How would she describe her motivation?
'I want to do something meaningful; that provides me with fulfilment. Wealth is not only about money – millionaires are not always happy; it's important for people to recognise that. My faith drives me to adding value to the community.'

And how does the business work?
'We are a limited company. As a Social Enterprise our profits go back into the company rather than going to shareholders. But we still have to operate as a commercial enterprise and balance heart and head. We don't run on grants, we have to be sustainable.

We operate in an open market; there are competitors so we have to offer a unique service. We currently deliver 500 hours of homecare services per week, respite education service during the term time, enterprise development sessions on a weekly basis and parenting support sessions.'

Where will the company go now?
'There is a pub nearby being closed down. We want to acquire the premises and upscale our activities, especially with the young.

We identify what's lacking and try to fill those gaps. My belief is, "If you don't see a door, make your own". My work gives me peace of mind.'

The rural business

❝ *I recently moved into offices having worked from home for the best part of 20 years. The reason is that I am fast approaching empty nest and felt vulnerable in my home in the countryside.* ❞
Karen Purves, Centre for Effective Marketing

Women are at the heart
There is an idyllic image of moving to the countryside and setting up a business, but the traditional agricultural base has been severely challenged over recent decades. It's probably true to say that the rural business sector is now far more diverse than it was 20 years ago, and women are very much part of that change.

❝ *55% of rural businesses operate from home compared with 39% of urban businesses.* ❞
Dwelly et al., 2006[25]

❝ *Home-based businesses play a key role in the sustainability of rural communities and small towns by reducing out-commuting, revitalising the daytime economy and adding to local purchasing.* ❞
Newbery and Bosworth, 2008[26]

Women in Rural Business (WiRE)
WiRE started in 1996 with a piece of research into falling farm incomes and diversification. Over the years, and in response to feedback from rural businesswomen, WiRE has developed a full business support package for women across the UK wanting to develop and grow their rural business.

Diversify in a beleaguered sector

CASE STUDY
Dove Farm, owned and run by Jane and Henry Stretton
www.dovefarm.co.uk
Business: working family farm and holiday cottages in Derbyshire

Jane describes herself as the townie who married a farmer and they have been through everything that the often beleaguered farm sector can throw at them. With a background in teaching and business, she now works to develop a diversified and sustainable rural enterprise. She tells how, as their plans for change came about, they were plunged into crisis:

'We took over the farm from Henry's father in 1995 and it is a very different business now. It is a relatively small scale farm so we always knew we would have to expand or diversify. It's just that circumstances forced our hand and we started on the diversification route quicker than we had anticipated.

One year into being a farmer's wife I was without my well-paid job because a temporary contract had not been renewed. The week that I came home from hospital with our new baby I received a phone call to say that my husband was on his way to A&E because of a farming-related accident. He was unable to work for nearly a year, with no sick pay (being self employed). All of this called for some major decision making – and quickly.

The best option, as we wanted to stay at the farm, was to convert the dairy buildings into three holiday cottages. This was totally dependent on obtaining European rural development funding and we were fortunate enough to achieve that. Our contingency plan was to sell up.

We borrowed heavily to raise our part of the finance and building work began in 1999. Part way through the Foot and Mouth crisis struck in 2001.

Like all farms, we were shut down, including building work. Thankfully we kept infection away from the farm (the nearest reported case was only three miles away). The downside of that is that we received no compensation for loss of livestock. Nor could we claim for any lost income from tourism because that part of the business was not yet up and running!'

What got them through it?
'We hung on with grim determination really and opened our holiday cottages in 2002. We were still paying off debts and crisis loans for years after. We now have three children and when they were small they were my incentive to diversify. I don't see the point of going out to work to do a job that you don't enjoy, to pay for the childcare that enables you to go to work. There's no doubt we have made a lifestyle choice rather than an economic one and it's a choice that our children don't always agree with, as they get older and see the different lifestyles that their friends have. I have no regrets about the choices we made and I'm always looking for new ventures and new initiatives to help the business move forward.'

How has the business developed?
'On turnover the division is around 60/40: farming/cottages. Profit is more difficult to separate as the asset value and operating costs of the cottages are part of the overall farming business.

It is also important to say that, essential as business plans are, the shape and focus of our business now bears no resemblance to the plans we made. We designed and marketed each cottage to be hired out separately, aimed at the disabled market. Now we hire out all three units together and our marketing is geared towards short breaks for larger groups and special occasion weekends.

I describe what we do as a value-led business. We are not competing with the spas and luxury resorts nor with the cut-price budget breaks for group holidays. We provide the right environment for guests to celebrate their special times and to spend a few days with the people they care about.'

What advice does she give to anyone planning a rural business?
'At the planning stage a rural business is no different to setting out on any kind of enterprise journey. You have to see if it "fits" in terms of everything else going on in your life and be as rigorous as you can in working out its financial viability.

Once your business venture is real and happening my advice is to "try it on for size" and if it doesn't "fit" any more, be prepared to change things or change direction. This is not defeat, it's just a fact of life, and being flexible and open to change could mean the difference between business success or failure.'

And what plans do the Strettons have?
'I am spending some time on diversifying myself now! I am training as a coach to pull together the skills I have gained over the years in business and education. I am confident that a strategy will emerge as I get a feel for what aspects of coaching I want to specialise in. Henry is concentrating on his farm machinery sales and is currently developing a website to support this enterprise.

I think it is important to "stay connected and in touch" with other businesses and other people doing things differently to you. The big danger with running your own business is that you become too inward looking, which can be unhelpful in staying motivated.

I am a local network leader for WIRE (Women in Rural Enterprise) and am delighted to provide facilities at the farm for network meetings and small events. I love the buzz and the energy from working with like-minded people. I find it immensely rewarding to share ideas and seek solutions within a trusted group, rather than feel completely on your own.'

Summary checklist: Change of life ventures

✔ If employment is proving too difficult it could be time to consider working for yourself.
✔ Consider setting up a home-based business.
✔ Take your business seriously, even at home.
✔ Get inspiration from other mums.
✔ Seek out the right help for you.
✔ Be tenacious – don't give up!
✔ Don't let your age deter you.
✔ Work around your disability.
✔ Consider buying a franchise if you have the funds.
✔ Look into direct selling.
✔ If community is important, think about a social enterprise.
✔ Diversify or change if you are under pressure.
✔ Network, especially if isolated.

Part 5
Growing Your Business

Introduction

' Women are half as likely to start a business as men. And they are more likely to stop along the way. '

Rebecca Harding, Managing Director, Delta Economics

Every business develops; they simply can't stay the same. Markets move on, tastes and fashions come and go, economies shrink and boom, and people's circumstances change. So no business is likely to be exactly the same even two years after launch. But some women drive this change. They establish a business with the goal of growing big. In this final section, you'll find some of the questions you need to consider before you become a big (or even a medium) shot.

We'll look at the opportunities to grow a business; the support you need; raising finance; and what the government and other agencies are doing to develop female-led businesses in the UK. There are people out there wanting to help you to greater success, so much of this section comes from them.

This is only a toe in the water. The Appendix has sources of support and finance and there are plenty of books for further reading. But firstly, let's explore the question . . .

CHAPTER TWENTY EIGHT

HAVE YOU GOT WHAT IT TAKES?

The majority of self-employed women stay small and don't employ anyone. And if that's what you want to do and it's your comfort zone, let's take the pressure off:

❝ *For many women it is an active choice to stay as a small business, as their motivations and drivers for enterprise more often feature quality of life, work/life balance, client satisfaction, freedom and control. We shouldn't infer, as too often happens, that there is something "wrong" with women because they make these choices. Growing a substantial business (say over £1 million annual turnover) usually requires a relentless determination, with long hours and frequent absences from home.* ❞

Bev Hurley, Founder and Chief Executive of Enterprising Women

❝ *It probably sounds strange but I have no desire to expand. I suppose it is classed as a lifestyle business. Expansion would mean premises, higher overheads, employing staff: stress and worry.* ❞

Jackie Roberts, The Chocolate Tailor

However, many female-led businesses have potential, so perhaps you are ready to take a step further.

Analyse what might hold you back

❝ *The data suggests that women are more likely (than men) to drop out as their business grows. Research has shown that women often leave their businesses because they are pursuing other interests or because they go back into employment.* ❞

Rebecca Harding, Managing Director, Delta Economics

❝ *Women tend to be more risk averse. I think it must come from the attitudes and beliefs we grew up with; about what our potential is as women. Maybe we have been told to be wary of risk, or to fear getting out of control.*

There is also a culture in the UK that it's ok to grow your own job, but it's not ok to have a business that grows (for women, at least). Thankfully, this belief is being broken down and girls are open to the concept of entrepreneurship. Attitudes are moving towards being in business rather than just being self employed. **❯**

Gill Fennings-Monkman, Director of Prowess and Consultant Director of Newham Women's Business Centre

❛ *Plenty of women do have the ambition and aspiration to grow their business but are held back by other factors. These include lack of confidence and self-belief, and lack of the right knowledge and skills; this is exacerbated by the lack of women-friendly growth programmes across the UK, and the generally inadequate quality of free public sector enterprise support when it comes to markets and sales.* **❯**

Bev Hurley, Founder and Chief Executive of Enterprising Women

So there's the challenge! You have got through your first year successfully and you can see potential in your businesses. But you know the next stage won't be easy. You will move into an arena of risk and finance much greater than you have experienced up to now. However, sometimes it doesn't do any harm to challenge ourselves and ask, 'Could I grow this business?'

❛ *36% of women running younger businesses (2–5 years) said their business had grown faster than they expected.* **❯**

COGS 2009[27]

Why grow?

- It's in the plan.
- To become a millionaire.
- Potential in the business.
- New information/research.
- Runaway success.
- Won a major contract/customer.
- Confidence/enthusiasm grows.
- Opportunity to buy competitor(s).
- Finance becomes available.
- Partner/influencer joins.
- Change in market.
- Change in your circumstances.

- Launching a new product.
- Diversifying.
- Exporting potential.

The determining factors:

- potential for profitable growth (scaleability)
- your preparedness to run a bigger business (risk, lifestyle etc.)
- your outlook and ability to adapt
- support
- finance.

Some strategies for growth

- Organic growth (more of the same)
- New product/diversification
- Franchise or set up direct selling distribution network
- Merger or acquisition
- Focusing on core/most profitable product (stick to the knitting).

Expand by franchising

CASE STUDY

Kiddy Cook Franchising Ltd, set up and being developed by Nikki Geddes
www.kiddycook.co.uk
Business: Expansion vehicle for Kiddy Cook, offering cookery classes and parties for children

Kiddy Cook is one of those neat little local businesses that would fulfil many people's ambition. Nikki started it four years ago when she moved from London to Cheshire for her husband's job. She had worked in broadcast journalism and marketing in London.

Nikki enjoys cooking and saw both benefit and opportunity in teaching children about cooking good food. However, it inevitably has geographic limitations. Even if Nikki subcontracted, she would need to be able to monitor clients and quality. Her goal is to develop a national business and she is doing that by franchising. Nikki explains why:

'Once I'd had my children I wanted a job that addressed the challenges of balancing fulfilling, flexible work with family life, while also generating a good income for part time work. I had always enjoyed cooking and loved baking with my daughter (then nearly three) so I decided to set up Kiddy Cook. I wasn't fearful about setting up the business because I started out on a very ad hoc basis, with a "suck it and see" approach. Kiddy Cook had relatively low set-up costs and no overheads so it was always in the back of my mind that I would have "nothing to lose" if things didn't work out. However, I did start out with a "friend" and there was a definite comfort factor having someone to hold your hand.'

How did she research the idea?
'I started out with a trial session and this proved very popular, with almost 95% repeat bookings. I also did straw poll research among family and friends to gauge interest and potential charges.'

What was her greatest challenge/threat?
'Self-motivation has been my biggest threat. I don't find it easy working from home, as there is always something else to do. It's also very hard to be inspired when working alone and I am very aware of the need to be around others to bounce around ideas with.'

What made her decide to expand rather than just carry on in her own area?
'It was always my view to franchise Kiddy Cook, right from the start. Rather naively, I didn't give it any real thought, I just had a "gut" feel that it was a business that could be replicated nationally and I used this as my basis for moving forward. I think because there was no real monetary risk involved I had a bit of a laissez faire approach to franchising. I took the view that if it worked, great and if not, I hadn't lost anything.'

What made her decide to expand by franchising? What advice did she get on how to do it?
'With regards to advice, initially I read books and looked online for information on franchising and I also requested information packs from other children's franchisees to see what they were offering. Last year, through networking, I made contact with a retired franchise lawyer. He really gave me the impetus to "go for it" as well as highlighting my own strengths and weaknesses. This was totally by chance.'

How did she judge the income stream?
'Again, I naively looked at my drawings per month and used them as a starting point for franchisees. It is only now that I have my accountant putting together some analysis for potential franchisees using my own figures. If I was starting the process again I would definitely incorporate this into my business plan as it was pure "luck" that things have worked out the way they have.'

How does she weigh up the pros and cons of this route (so far)?
'Although I have been talking about franchising Kiddy Cook since its conception, I have only really "focused" since my son started school full-time in 2008. The pros are seeing other people running with my idea and beginning to turn it into a successful business for themselves. That's a real confidence boost and makes me feel very proud. The downside is the amount of work required to help turn somebody else's business into a reality.'

What is the balance of time spent between expansion and her original business?
'Initially I wanted to keep my "area" but I don't have the time to develop both of them properly. As a result, I plan to sell part of my business as a franchise. I will keep some of the classes as I think it's important for me to be "on the ground" to ensure that what I propose works for other franchisees.

My work/life balance has changed since franchising my business. I anticipate that as more franchisees come on board the time spent franchising will increase but I am using my time now to ensure that I have everything in place. As the business develops I'll have a lot less time to call my own and this goes against why I set up in business in the first place. But I'm ready for a new challenge and feel confident that I can organise my time to have quality time at home.'

Develop a brand through a franchise

CASE STUDY
Musical Minis established and run by Karen Sherr
Business: the franchising of music groups for babies and children up to pre-school age

Karen set up Musical Minis in 1989, mainly to provide the right kind of musical class for her young children. With a number of successful classes locally she and her husband (who works part time in the business) decided to franchise the operation in 1996. She takes up the story:

'I was previously a play specialist on the cardiac unit at Great Ormond Street Children's Hospital and I had stopped work to bring up my first child. I began Musical Minis when my first child was a baby because I could not find what I wanted for my son in the area. We went to an exercise group where the children sang songs and the singing was his favourite part of the class.

We opened a number of local groups over seven years and the operation was profitable. I had customers who had moved away contacting me and asking if I could open a class in their area. We had always had expansion at the back of our minds, so this seemed the right time.

Now we had to get more serious. We had to pay for the recording of the music, the trade mark and other set-up costs, so we did have to analyse the risks. We took legal advice to set up the agreement. We developed the strategy and business plan, with financial projections, ourselves.'

What gave her the impetus to expand?
'My husband Rob is a commercial banker and he is responsible for the finance. He could see how the business could grow and that the franchise we offered was sound; so I had security in his financial acumen. I'm not sure I would have done that alone.'

Why did they choose franchising?
'It seemed the right way to expand. I didn't know how else I could find people, and beyond the London and SouthEast I didn't know the area. Giving someone a franchise means that with our support they take responsibility for the business's success in an area where they have knowledge.'

What do they offer the franchisee?
'We have a business plan and tailored projections to demonstrate how the franchisee could grow the business. It was set up properly, so we have a legally drafted agreement which is balanced between franchisor and franchisee, as it should be. It details everyone's responsibilities.

We don't set the franchisee targets; instead we let them build their business as they wish. Some are mums with young children who just want to do a few hours, while others work 30 hour weeks and have staff under them.

They receive training in our programme and report back termly with their figures. We keep a close eye on how every business is doing. I don't employ anyone, but some of the franchisees are regional managers who do training and make periodic visits to franchisees for quality checks and support. We recently appointed a regional manager for Scotland so that they could support the existing franchisee and expand that region.'

Has she had any problems with franchisees?
'No disasters, but one franchisee took over a successful operation and ran it down. She thought she knew better and changed the format to music classes, whereas we see them as child development with music. She lost a lot of customers and in the end she closed it down. If she hadn't, we have a clause in the contract where we can withdraw a franchise.'

How has the business developed?
'We now have 19 franchises plus 15 licences in Sure Start Centres, which run our programme. The annual turnover is £100,000. I've always put the family first, which has kept expansion in check. Now that my family is grown we are at a stage where it can be a bigger business, so we are looking for more franchisees.

All our growth has been self-funded. That was something my husband felt was imperative.

We joined the British Franchise Association two years ago. It is expensive, but they scrutinize all our plans and agreements, so potential franchisees can have confidence in us. We think this will help our future expansion.'

CHAPTER TWENTY NINE

GOING FOR GROWTH

❝ If a woman has a dedicated approach to the business, success is non-negotiable. She often says, "I've found a glass ceiling; I'm determined to break through it". They are similar to their male counterparts; they have a clear sense of strategy. They find ways of matching their femininity with hard business imperatives. ❞

Rebecca Harding, Managing Director, Delta Economics

Finding support

❝ Delegate. Get the key skills in so that you can manage the business. Women aren't very good at doing this; we think we ought to be doing it all. But you've got to step back emotionally when you grow; it's not your baby any more. ❞

Elizabeth Gooch, Chief Executive, eg solutions plc

Earlier in the book we saw how the freelance and micro business had to build a team of trusted suppliers around it: IT, finance, design, marketing. Then it was outsourced and led by the chief: you. So even with that support, you had to be involved and probably implement much of it. As the business grows further, these functions move in-house, and as the business upscales, you need more senior people to head these functions. Without losing touch, you need to find those capable and trusted people who have the same goals as you.

What support do you need?

Support	Where from
Planning: in the beginning you need to know if your plans could work and you may need help to restructure.	Business adviser such as one of the women's support services, below; investor or consultant.
Advisory: a key, right hand person for strategic advice and help with decision making.	This could be a mentor, non-executive board member, finance director (read the Case Studies to see who these women have).

IT: even if you are not in an IT business, most businesses use IT. It is crippling if the website, production, purchasing or billing systems go down. Make sure you have capable and fast response.

At some point you will move your outsourcing in-house so that you have an IT support and development team – yes, your very own geeks! As you grow bigger you may well outsource some of the functions again, possibly overseas.

Financial: you will need to do financial plans, source finance, possibly take on equity partners and keep a very tight grip on operating finances.

If you are not confident about figures and finance, now is the time to get savvy. Get good advice about growth finance and a finance director you can really work with. But you must still understand how your business finances operate.

Marketing: this is a function in which you may have a more hands-on role. You have lived and breathed the product for a few years; you may well have created it. Your personality is behind it and you will still be a great asset with customers.

All the same, you will now need marketing and sales. Like IT, you may bring them in-house, and then outsource certain parts, such as advertising, PR and design campaigns.

Human resources: you may have done your own hiring and firing to date, perhaps with an outsourced payroll function. Now it will be time to bring this in-house.

Like all these functions, you may start with one person. HR is now highly specialist requiring not just 'people' skills: they need knowledge of employment law, using recruiters and head hunters, interview and selection, training, career development, appraisals and redundancy and dismissal. People will be your best resource: get someone good.

Legal: at this level, your contracts have to be watertight – staff, suppliers, customers. There is a lot of UK and European legislation you have to comply with and, sadly, you probably won't be in business for long before you have some litigation.

Most businesses hire lawyers from outside initially, then employ them as in-house counsel when they grow. You know you've arrived if you have one of them!

Appointing external advisers and suppliers

Hold a pitch, or 'beauty parade'

Nowadays, everyone expects to tender, or pitch, for business. So draw up a brief, being very specific about what you want, how you want it done, what results you would like and what kind of people you like working with. Even City lawyers can be hip these days. Don't be surprised if *they tell you* want you want and what results to expect; if they are credible it shows confidence and creativity.

Set your criteria

Be tough on fees, but don't necessarily appoint the team that comes in cheapest. Make sure that the individuals you meet and impress you are the ones who are going to be doing your work, or at least be very involved in the strategy. Don't necessarily go for the local team down the road as nowadays you can work with people anywhere in the world, as long as there is a cultural fit. Just make sure you feed them well when they visit for meetings.

Get the right fit

You can source all suppliers from directories, websites, word-of-mouth and your own in-house specialists' recommendations. Make sure they are not so big that you will be small fry to them (you'll get their attention in recession but maybe not when things are booming). Equally, make sure they have the capacity and specialist skills to take you on.

Financing growth

❝ *Women invest as much in their businesses at start-up as men: it took entrepreneurs on average £105,000 to start their business irrespective of gender, and women and men alike invest just over 70% of this from their own resources.*

...This money predominantly comes from savings or current accounts... External finance...comes principally from the bank in the form of overdrafts or loans, but women are four times more likely to access government grants compared to men. ❞

COGS 2009[28]

Where will you get your money from? If you have never borrowed beyond family and friends or have rubbed along with a bank loan or overdraft, the next stage could take you into the heady world of high finance: grants, venture capital, equity partners and business angels. You will have to do your homework.

Sources of finance

Sources

Bank loan: we've heard tales of women rejected by banks, but the research shows this is more perception than fact. Women may be charged higher rates because they borrow lower amounts.

Venture capital: sometimes called private equity. Venture capitalists (VCs) run funds that invest in start-up or growth. companies. In 2004, companies with female CEOs received only 2.5% of all venture capital funding.

Business angel: wealthy private investors, often with knowledge of a particular sector and looking to 'get on board' and help.

Public listing: this is for the big timers and most small companies don't list on either exchange (AIM or the Stock Market). If you have friends and family who have made loans, you could consider converting this to shares. You should get legal and financial advice before you do this.

Pros and cons

Terms vary; it remains 100% in your ownership. Establish a good working relationship with your bank and make sure they understand your business.

Equity finance is not a loan so you do not pay interest nor have a fixed term to repay. Instead they will look for dividend payments, like shareholders; often some control of the business; and a share when it is sold or floats. They usually bring managerial and technical expertise as well as capital. Always get financial advice before taking on private equity.

This is more of a personal relationship (notice the hugs and handshakes on *Dragon's Den*). You can have a group of angels and they may invest as a loan or as equity. Make sure you have rapport – you'll be seeing a lot of them!

There are very few female led companies listed on AIM (the Alternative Investment Market), but that's not to say you won't be there one day. See the Case Study on Elizabeth Gooch, below.

Remember, *you* want them to think your business is the best thing since Microsoft. And they might. But *they* also want a good return on their money.

Is equity finance right for you?

❝ Different forms of equity finance suit different business situations.

It is likely to be most suitable where:
- *the nature of a project deters debt providers, e.g., banks*
- *the business will not have enough cash to pay loan interest because it is needed for core activities or funding growth*

Questions to ask yourself include:
- *Are you prepared to give up a share in your business and some control? Investors expect to monitor progress and many seek involvement in significant decisions.*
- *Are you and your key people confident in the business's product/ service? Does it have a unique selling point that singles it out?*
- *Do you have the drive to grow the business?*
- *What industry experience and knowledge does your management team have? Is there a variety of skills?*

Remember that, because of the risk to their funds, investors expect a higher potential return than for safer, more secure investments. ❞

Business Link website: *Equity finance*

❝ Getting financing involves knowing banks, investors etc., which means men (more than 90% of VCs are men). And investors tend to invest in entrepreneurs they know. In the natural business and social network of a man, there are obviously more men; just as in the business and social network of women, there are more women. So women have to take extra steps to get to know those male investors.

The Next Woman helps them with this. There are a lot of women who are financially independent, but those women have not yet become angel investors. We are working on that as well with The Next Woman. ❞

Simone Brummelhuis, founder of thenextwoman.com

Grow a business by acquisition

CASE STUDY
Oberoi Consulting, established and developed by managing director Kavita Oberoi www.oberoi-consulting.com
www.kavitaoberoi.com
Business: clinical audit and IT training; business consulting for GP practices

Kavita Oberoi runs a very successful UK company based in Derby. She gained fame following her appearance in 2008 on Channel Four's Secret Millionaire. *She left a successful career with a multinational pharmaceutical company and broke through family boundaries to become a female entrepreneur in 2001. Her accolades are now too numerous to mention here, but they include the NRI Pride of India Gold Award in 2005 and Fellowship of the RSA. She has found that success breeds success both personally and for her business. She grabs a moment from a busy schedule to talk:*

'I had applied for promotion while on maternity leave with my second child. I didn't get it. All kinds of reasons about my abilities were given, and I felt I hadn't had a chance to demonstrate them. I realised even in another job I would have to work eight or ten years before someone else told me I could do it. I had confidence in myself and I knew I had the skills and the training to be a success.

So I decided to set up on my own and I identified the opportunity: training doctors to use their clinical systems better to identify patients for screening and preventative treatment. This combined my pharmaceutical experience and my IT abilities.

When I left, I had been earning £35,000, so I simply thought, "How many days do I have to work to earn more?" I worked out that it would be about two days a week. The safety net was that I could always go back into a job if it didn't work out.

I worked from home to begin with. Other than stock, it didn't need any investment, so the earning potential convinced me it was the right thing to do.'

How did she grow the business?
'It progressed very quickly. I had Pfizer as my first client and other blue chip clients followed. The business has always been self-funding so there is no debt; that is down to my attitude to finance. Up until now, it has grown organically, taking the opportunities as they come.

The key is delivery: as long as we delivered successfully, it was ok. That's always been our advantage.'

What has happened to the business in 2010?
'I have bought shares in a global security company, Octavian Security.

The two companies combined will employ over 500 people and be based in our offices in Derby. I knew the owner of the business, who has grown it single handedly, organically, very like mine. The bank was pulling terms so it needed private equity and I thought this was a great business to grow and sell on. It's exciting and risky. But you have to take some risks.

Octavian also provides security to the healthcare industry, for instance lone-worker support, so there is a lot of synergy with Oberoi Consulting.'

What key characteristic does she need to be in business?
'A lot of focus and single minded dedication. This takes a lot of time and sacrifice and you have to be prepared to do that.

Business wise, I don't just chase for sales. Many companies are doing massive turnovers, but the bottom line is tiny. I focus on the profit.'

And one thing leads to another...
'Through *Secret Millionaire* I am supporting the *Sisters with Voices* programme, and devoting more time to charity work. My two daughters get involved as well. I am committed to helping young women and seeing them flourish. I have recently been asked to lead a campaign for the Girl Guides, to raise £10 million over the next five years. If it wasn't for running my business I could do charity work full time. The reward always comes back, when you see the impact you make. It gives me a fulfilment that is different from earning money.'

Take a company on to AIM

CASE STUDY
eg solutions plc, established and developed by chief executive Elizabeth Gooch www.eguk.co.uk
Business: AIM listed operations management software company, specialising in the financial services sector

Elizabeth Gooch is one of the country's most successful business women and one of the few female entrepreneurs heading an AIM listed company. She walked out from under the glass ceiling in 1988 when only 26 to start consulting and entered the mostly male world of finance and technology.

*She has had business and personal challenges, and it's not possible to do
full justice to her story here, but Elizabeth highlights some milestones:*

'I was working for a large building society and kept solving problems the
managers couldn't figure out. But they would only offer me assistant
manager position – at that time, there were few women in senior
positions and no women on the board. So I left and set up my own
business, initially in consulting.

The bank managers I approached at high street banks were old school;
they laughed at the thought of a 26-year-old woman running a business
offering advice to companies in financial services. I finally opened an
account with Co-operative Bank. I funded the launch with a loan of
£1,000 from friends and family and credit cards. Even after a year and
with a turnover of £700,000 I was still refused proper banking facilities.
But I see obstacles as challenges to be overcome.

In 1993 I developed a software package called Operational Intelligence,
employing six staff and several contract workers. The turnover built to
£4 million with a £400,000 overdraft. At that time I ran the business to
suit my lifestyle. If I went on holiday, the turnover went down; I was the
centre of everything, it revolved around me.'

What were her motivations and sacrifices?
'I've always been ambitious. I'm one of those people who are never
satisfied. From the start I aimed to build a business with a £10 million
turnover.

It has been my focus and I have earned a good lifestyle from it, but it
has cost me two marriages and a partnership. I probably worked harder
in the beginning than now – six or seven days a week – so my daughter
was raised by nannies. I do regret missing out on her childhood, but I'm
fortunate that she has turned out to be a fabulous daughter and we're
good friends.

Then in 2001 I was diagnosed with rheumatoid arthritis and was unable
to walk for three to six months. I still have it, but it's not as bad now. I
realised I had to change how I ran the business.'

What was the turning point?
'This was the point when I realised I didn't have to do, or control,

everything myself. I brought in Rodney Baker-Bates from Prudential Financial Services as chairman. We conducted a strategic review and he recommended that I should build into a "proper" business. The consultants suggested we should drop the consultancy and focus on the software. It was a unique product, and still is. It gave us better traction and from then our growth was 28% per annum.

Then in 2005 we needed more capital to grow, so we had two choices: venture capital or flotation on AIM (the smaller companies market). It had to be the latter, as I didn't want any investors with a large stake in the business dictating how we operate. It was very difficult when we didn't hit our targets in 2006/7. I took it very personally.'

What was the key lesson here?
'We rushed onto AIM and we should have spent more time on strategy and targets. But otherwise, there's nothing I would change.'

What is her view on working mothers?
'I honestly don't think many women can do this. Biology is biology and you have to make a choice. I was judged badly by my daughter's schools, because I was a working mother, always rushing around, forgetting the school bags and so on.

I think things have changed a lot in recent years. I don't think there is the same pressure to come back to work and there is greater choice. But there are also more enterprises that can be run from home nowadays and that can be both flexible and fulfilling.

However, if you have a good business and want to grow, I'd say "go for it". Get scale by not being at the centre of things and concentrate on working on the business.'

Where does she go from here?
'I want to rebuild the business, back up to £20 million capital value. Then I'm looking for an exit. I want to start another business in another field, like retail or leisure. I will simplify my life.'

CHAPTER THIRTY

WHAT HELP DO WOMEN ENTREPRENEURS NEED?

❛ *One day we hope there will be no need for specialist organisations or projects like this to help women starting and growing business. There will be widespread understanding and acceptance of the different approaches and motivations women often have to starting a business and managing its growth, and improved services for women and men alike.* ❜

Bev Hurley, Founder and Chief Executive of Enterprising Women

❛ *Support providers need to work with organisations like Prowess, which support women to create transformational change. We need more business centres, places to go, events to attend so that we can meet other like-minded women.* ❜

Gill Fennings-Monkman, Director of Prowess and Consultant Director of Newham Women's Business Centre

What a dedicated business centre can do

Newham Women's Business Centre

Newham College's Women's Business Centre in East London has won the Prowess Flagship of the Year Award. This confers its status as best provider of women's enterprise support in the country.

It is two years old and is the first purpose built business centre for women in the country. 83% of its clients are from ethnic minorities and 75% are self employed and work alone.

It is a place where women can go to get support and inspiration: bounce round an idea before preparing a business plan. Membership starts at £25 a year for coaching, training, workshops and other events.

(Website: www.herbusinessuk.co.uk Tel: 020 8257 4204)

West Midlands Women's Business Centre

The West Midlands Women's Business Centre, led by the Women's Business

Development Agency, is the first of the national women's business centres to be launched in the former government's Enterprise Strategy.

The Business Centre is designed to encourage more women to seriously consider setting up their own businesses by providing a wealth of expertise, help and online training to help them take the first crucial steps.

Business growth is also a major role of the West Midlands Women's Business Centre, providing effective and comprehensive business support, helping female entrepreneurs to take advantage of online training and mentoring to enable them to build their businesses.

(Website: www.wmwomensbusinesscentre.com Tel: 02476 236111)

What support is needed from government?

❛ They need to see that the job is not done yet. It has never been a more important time to keep the focus on women's enterprise. There has been so much investment in this country to bring us up to the US levels of activity. And there is still huge value from self-employment and small business to the economy. ❜

> Gill Fennings-Monkman, Director of Prowess and Consultant Director of
> Newham Women's Business Centre

There has been a lot of government-backed supportive work done through the first decade of this century. With the election in 2010 and public spending cuts there is much uncertainty over the future of this work.

That will be a pity as it has turned attention to addressing the specific issues that women face in establishing self employment or a business; the two business centres above have been established; Business Link had seminars tailored to women start-ups; finance has (in the past, at least) been ring-fenced for female led ventures and there has been a growth in women working for themselves.

A government-sponsored *Women's Enterprise Task Force*, which ran for three years to the end of 2009, noted that turnover from women-led, small and medium sized enterprises was estimated at £130 billion. In its final report it called for:

■ better research to coordinate and disseminate learning
■ more encouragement for women starting and growing businesses
■ an improvement in the environment for growth finance.

First indications from the coalition government are that this support won't now come from the public sector.

Find a mentor

Throughout this book we have seen the benefit to women of having someone to support them through challenging and often lonely times. This has been a husband or partner, an outside adviser or coach or a networking colleague.

The importance of such a person is recognised and many successful businesswomen now offer their time to inspire and mentor through networks, conferences and supportive schemes.

The key to your success, apart from your own sheer dedication, is to learn from others. Don't struggle alone or despair when you meet seemingly insurmountable obstacles. The chances are, there is someone in your town or region, or online who has gone through the same experience.

The momentum of women working for themselves is now unstoppable (even if there is a hiatus in government activity); the specialist help is there if you search and the networks are hugely supportive.

Be inspired, be brave and be successful!

Summary checklist: Growing your business

✓ Reflect on change for your business.
✓ Only grow if it is right for you.
✓ Look at the potential for growth.
✓ Build a strategy around expansion.
✓ Think about franchising.
✓ Delegate – build a team around you.
✓ Appoint advisers.
✓ Consider all the finance options.
✓ Get the right support.
✓ Pass on your experience.

PEARLS OF WISDOM

What's the best thing you've done?
I have built a support network: my business coach, PA, family, friends and networking colleagues.
Samantha Russell, Sardine Web Design

Recognised our potential and our need to make a difference.
Cherry Parsons, CJ Motor Repairs

Got feedback from peers and contacts. It gave me confidence and meaningful information to go in the right direction.
Emma Pearce, Pearce Marketing Consultants

Is there anything you wish you hadn't done?
I wish I hadn't taken on a business partner. A lack of confidence meant I felt more 'comfortable' with him as a 'cushion' and when things didn't work out I was left having to pay him a sum of money which I didn't have.
Nikki Geddes, Kiddy Cook Franchising

Signed up to put my business cards in Tesco for 2 years. I think that was £600 down the drain!
Emma Lodge, Balance Accounting Solutions

Spent money with a new distribution company, who completely let us down. They insisted on up-front payment and completely ripped us off! But all my experiences, whether bad or good, have been valuable and helped me develop myself and the business.
Kristina Thomas, Sussex Local Magazine

I arrived at a client to discover they actually needed a different job done than we had discussed. It wasn't my area of expertise, but I said I would give it a go. It took an entire day and was not successful, so I didn't feel that I could charge the client. I should have clarified and avoided getting into this situation. I need to learn to say, 'No'.
Mary Thomas, Concise Training

What was your greatest challenge?

Handing over responsibility for running groups to people I didn't know, often located a long way away. This requires a huge amount of trust. However, that is what franchising is all about. While occasionally things do go wrong, largely, we have recruited a fabulous bunch of people who are as dedicated to running the business as I am.

Karen Sherr, Musical Minis

Who was worth their weight in gold?

I've been lucky enough to have a lot of great advisers as well as friends who are in small businesses like mine and pass on tips. Different people give different advice; you have to learn to weigh up what people say and make your own decisions. But having that original input is invaluable.

Tabitha Harman, Mimimyne

My coaching/counselling supervisor, who saw me through my course and the start of my business. I have met some good Business Link advisers over the years, generally just for one or two sessions.

Janice Taylor, Blue Sky Career Consulting

A couple of inspirational speakers at a European conference. They said, 'Leap and the net will appear'; and, 'Chase your passion, not your pension'. Both these statements struck a chord. I remember also, Simon Woodruffe (of *Yo! Sushi*) saying, 'You must listen to the voice inside that says, "you can" not the voice that says, "you can't".'

Jackie Roberts, The Chocolate Tailor

How important is networking?

Networking is great but you have to be prepared to put in more than you get out to begin with; people have to trust you and then leads follow. Different groups have different dynamics and it's important to find one that fits your personality.

Corinne McLavy, Zero3 Marketing

I only network online and it is invaluable.

Lisa Cole, Lactivist

What key advice can you give?

1. If you have a gut-feeling but aren't able to articulate it, then take the time to get to the root of it. Remember, no one knows you or your business as well as you do.

2.   Take full responsibility for your finances. It is not your accountant's responsibility to ensure you make money. It's vital to understand how the profit and loss, balance sheet and cash flow tie up together.
3.   Your business is a reflection of you. If you see something you don't like, it is very tempting to blame it and to get angry with it. Instead, work on this within yourself and really understand what the issue is.

Kaye Taylor, SK Chase

1.   Don't worry about the sales – focus on the profit.
2.   Reputation is really, really important. Through reputation and delivery, you set your quality standards.
3.   You have to be prepared to make sacrifices.

Kavita Oberoi FRSA, Oberoi Consulting

Delegate. Get the key skills in so that you can manage the business. Women aren't very good at doing this; we think we ought to be doing it all. But you've got to step back emotionally when you grow; it's not your baby any more.

Elizabeth Gooch, eg solutions plc

Do something meaningful that provides you with fulfilment. Wealth is not only about money – millionaires are not always happy. It's important for people to recognise that.

Claudine Reid, MBE, PJs Community Services

Know yourself; know why you are starting and how you will end. It's important because sometimes people do things for the wrong reason and end up chasing a dream that isn't theirs. Trust and believe in yourself, be prepared to be the *only* one swimming upstream. Plan to win and trust your gut feeling and instinct; they cannot be ignored.

Yana Johnson MBE, Yana Cosmetics

APPENDIX: USEFUL CONTACTS AND SUPPORT

Business support

Business Link: Free government-backed business advice network (see endnote) www.businesslink.gov.uk

Business Link in London: women's online centre www.bllondon.com/women/

Enterprise UK: Information and support for anyone starting up in business. www.enterpriseuk.org

NFEA National Enterprise Network: information and regional groups www.nfea.com

The Federation of Small Businesses: membership organisation supporting self employed and business owners www.fsa.org.uk

Business Startup Community: advice and links www.startupcommunity.co.uk

British Chambers of Commerce: national network supporting the business community www.britishchambers.org.uk Find your local chamber

England's Regional Development Agencies: responsible for spreading economic prosperity across nine regions of England www.englandsrdas.com

Women's business and networking organisations

Prowess:the UK association of organisations and individuals who support the growth of women's business ownership www.prowess.org.uk

The Women's Business Clubs: national support and networking www.thewomensbusinessclubs.com

Everywoman: advice, tools and networking for your business www.everywoman.com

Women in Business Network: for professional women and women entrepreneurs www.wibn.co.uk

The Next Woman: for female internet heroes www.thenextwoman.com

Women's Wisdom: helps people in the South of England improve their life chances www.womenswisdom.co.uk

The Women's Business Centre, East London: award-winning centre of business support www.herbusiness.co.uk

Women's Business Development Agency: helps women in the West Midlands start and grow their business www.wbda.co.uk

West Midlands Women's Business Centre: start-up and business support for women in the West Midlands www.wmwomensbusinesscentre.com

National Black Women's Network: champions the advancement of women across all professional disciplines www.nbwn.org

Women Unlimited: information and support for female entrepreneurs www.women-unlimited.co.uk

Enterprising Women: for women starting and growing a business in East Anglia www.enterprising-women.org

Women into the Network: supporting business women in the north east www.womenintothenetwork.co.uk

SouthEast Women's Enterprise Networks: supporting women in the south east www.womensenterprisesoutheast.co.uk

Women in Business: support and networking for women in Northern Ireland www.womeninbusinessni.com

Mumpreneurs

The Mumpreneur Directory www.mumpreneurdirectory.com

Mum's Club www.mumsclub.co.uk

The Mumpreneur Guide: guide to starting your own business www.mumpreneurguide.co.uk

Mums in Control: magazine for working and self-employed mothers www.mumsincontrol.co.uk

Ethnic communities

Itzcaribbean: information and resources for the UK Caribbean community www.itzcaribbean.com click business

The Asian Business Federation: trade and membership organisation for the UK Asian community www.abfed.co.uk

Coaching and mentoring

Available from a number of agencies. Search the internet for private providers. Sandra Hewett www.shmr.co.uk

Other SME websites

Enterprise UK: gives people confidence to set up in business www.enterpriseuk.org/home

Real Business Magazine: for entrepreneurs www.realbusiness.co.uk/news/business-woman

Growing Business Magazine: for growing businesses www.growingbusiness.co.uk

Smarta: advice and networking resource www.smarta.com

Small Business UK: information for small businesses www.smallbusiness.co.uk

Enterprise Nation: resource to help you start and grow your business from home

www.enterprisenation.com
Startups: website inspiring new business www.startups.co.uk
Is 4 profit: free small business advice and information www.is4profit.com/

Freelance
www.freelanceuk.com offers freelance insurance
www.freelancer.co.uk

Homeworking
Homeworking UK: internet homeworking directory www.homeworkinguk.com

The serious stuff
Companies House: the official UK government register of UK companies
www.companieshouse.gov.uk
Business Link: business support, information and advice www.businesslinkgov.uk.
Go to Starting up, business names and structures, legal structures
HM Revenue and Customs: tax, National Insurance and VAT registration
www.hmrc.gov.uk/startingup

Working for only one person or firm
If you are going to be working for one person or firm, you may not be able to
become self employed. For more information you can call the Self Assessment
Helpline on Tel 0845 9000 444

Health and safety
Health and Safety Executive www.hse.gov.uk See *An Introduction to Health and
Safety* (reprinted 2008)

Intellectual property
Intellectual Property Office: can help you get the right type of protection for
your creation or invention www.ipo.gov.uk

Commercial property
Royal Institution of Chartered Surveyors www.rics.org/uk

Business Rates
Valuation Office Agency www.2010.voa.gov.uk/rli

Data protection agency
www.ico.gov.uk

Insurance

A guide to protect your business, www.abi.org.uk

Legal/find a solicitor

Law Society www.lawsociety.org.uk

Finance/find an accountant

The Institute of Chartered Accountants www.icaewfirms.co.uk

Finance

Business Link www.businesslink.gov.uk Go to finance and grants.

Department of Business Innovation and Skills www.bis.gov.uk Go to Enterprise and Support, Access to Finance

HM Revenue and Customs www.hmrc.gov.uk for tax, National Insurance and VAT. Includes a guide to working for yourself (all you need to know about registering for tax when becoming self-employed – don't ignore this!).

Asset Based Finance Association: trade association for members supplying liquidity to UK businesses www.abfa.org.uk

Fair Finance Consortium: helping businesses in the West Midlands with finance www.fair-finance.net

West Midlands finance: as above www.westmidlandsfinance.com

Trapezia VC fund: www.stargatecapital.co.uk

British Business Angels Association: promotes angel investing and supports early stage investment in the UK www.bbaa.org.uk

Angel-Investors: brings together private investors (business angels) and entrepreneurs looking for funding www.angel-investors.co.uk

Marketing

CanDoCanBe: attracting new clients www.candocanbe.com

Market research

The Market Research Society www.mrs.org.uk
The Research Buyer's Guide www.rbg.org.uk

Social Media

How to use Twitter for Business www.havemoreclients.com

Public Relations

Chartered Institute of Public Relations www.cipr.co.uk
Public Relations Consultants Association www.prca.org.uk

Advertising

Institute of Practitioners in Advertising www.ipa.co.uk

Networking/social marketing

Twitter: messaging in the here-and-now www.twitter.com
LinkedIn: international networking for professionals www.linkedin.com

Community support

Fredericks Foundation: a charity that offers loans to people in the south of England who cannot access other channels of funding www.fredericksfoundation.org

In Biz: programme part-funded by the London Development Agency offering access to funding to the unemployed, ex offenders and disability benefit claimants www.inbiz.co.uk

Crisis Changing Lives: a grant scheme helping single homeless people get into work or self employment www.crisis.org.uk. Search employment, changing lives.

Startup: a charity that offers ex-offenders the opportunity to become self-employed www.startupnow.org.uk

Head for Business: London-based Community Interest company that helps the young and socially excluded to work for themselves www.head4biz.com

Youth

Shell Livewire www.shell-livewire.org
The Prince's Trust www.princes-trust.org.uk
The National Council for Youth Entrepreneurship www.ncge.com
flying start: helping students and graduates get businesses started (run by NCGE) www.flyingstartonline.com
The National Enterprise Academy: full time education programme in enterprise for 16–19 year olds, set up by Dragon's Den Peter Jones www.thenea.org

Rural

Women into Rural Enterprise: UK networking and business club for rural women www.wireuk.org

Disability

Leonard Cheshire Disability: www.lcdisability.org
Queen Elizabeth's Foundation: provides training for adults with disabilities www.qefd.org

ENHAM: helps disabled people create opportunities and change www.enham.org.uk

Northern Pinetree Trust: helps people with a long term illness or disability www.northernpinetreetrust.co.uk

Franchising
British Franchise Association: voluntary, self governing body for franchising www.thebfa.org

Direct selling distributors
Direct Selling Association: national trade association for businesses selling directly to consumers www.dsa.org. Has guide about tax and accounting.

Social Enterprise
Social Enterprise Coalition: the UK's national body for social enterprise www.socialenterprise.org.uk

The Social Investment Business: grants for social enterprises working in health and social care www.socialinvestmentbusiness.org

Older people
Prime Initiative: UK charity that helps people over 50 set up in business; founded by the Prince of Wales www.primebusinessclub.co.uk

Endnote:
At the time of going to press the government has announced the closure of Business Link, to be replaced by an online support service. Other public sector and quango agencies may also be affected.

REFERENCES

Chapter 2
1. *Putting the economy back on track: Work-Life Balance* (2008), Federation of Small Businesses. A survey of members, www.fsb.org.uk, p19

Chapter 11
2. Patten, D (2001) *Successful Marketing for the Small Business*. London: Kogan Page, p191

Chapter 13
3. Survey of female entrepreneurs commissioned by the then Minister for Women and Equality, Harriet Harman. Research was conducted online by YouGov between 30 April and 7 May 2008. YouGov interviewed a sample of 1,026 UK women who have started their own business
4, 5. Women's Enterprise and Access to Finance, National Policy Centre for Women's Enterprise Evidence Paper, Professor Sara Carter, University of Strathclyde, March 2009, p3
www.prowesspolicycentre.org.uk/accesstofinance
6. *Stairways to Growth 2010*, Delta Economics www.deltaeconomics.com, p10

Chapter 18
7. *Women's Enterprise and Access to Finance*, National Policy Centre for Women's Enterprise Evidence Paper, Professor Sara Carter, University of Strathclyde, March 2009, p2, www.prowesspolicycentre.org.uk/accesstofinance
8. *Myths and Realities of Women's Access to Finance*, report commissioned by the Women's Enterprise Task Force and researched by Dr Rebecca Harding of Delta Economics, July 2009, www.womensenterprisetaskforce.co.uk
9. Quoting: Shaw, Carter *et al.* (2005) *Social Capital and Accessing Finance: The Relevance of Networks*. Paper presented at the 28th Institute for Small Business Entrepreneurship National Conference, Blackpool, 2005

Chapter 19
10. *Putting the economy back on track: Work-Life Balance*, (2008) Federation of Small Businesses. A survey of members, www.fsb.org.uk, p20

Chapter 20
11. *How to use Twitter for Business*, Karen Purves, www.havemoreclients.com, p7

Chaper 24
12. *Putting the economy back on track: Work-Life Balance*, (2008) Federation of Small Businesses. A survey of members www.fsb.org.uk, p13
13. Carter, S, Mason, C and Tagg, S (2009) *Invisible Businesses: The Characteristics of Home-based Businesses in the UK*. University of Strathclyde: The Hunter Centre for Entrepreneurship, pp23, 40
14. Carter, S, Mason, C and Tagg, S (2009) *Invisible Businesses: The Characteristics of Home-based Businesses in the UK*. University of Strathclyde: The Hunter Centre for Entrepreneurship, p5
15. *Putting the economy back on track: Work-Life Balance* (2008), Federation of Small Businesses. A survey of members www.fsb.org.uk p7

Chapter 26
16. Business Link: see starting a business on a low income, www.businesslink.gov.uk
17. *The Corston Report: a review of women with particular vulnerabilities in the criminal justice system* (2007)
18. Carter, S, Mason, C and Tagg, S (2009) *Invisible Businesses: The Characteristics of Home-based Businesses in the UK*. University of Strathclyde: The Hunter Centre for Entrepreneurship, p25
19. Carter, S, Mason, C and Tagg, S (2009) *Invisible Businesses: The Characteristics of Home-based Businesses in the UK*. University of Strathclyde: The Hunter Centre for Entrepreneurship, p24
20. www.lcdisability.org/enabled4enterprise
21. *Putting the economy back on track: Work-Life Balance*, (2008), Federation of Small Businesses. A survey of members www.fsb.org.uk, p5

Chapter 27
22 www.thebfa.org/aboutfranchising
23. British Franchise Association: *How to choose a franchise*, www.thebfa.org/joiningafranchise
24. www.socialenterprise.org.uk/pages/what-is-social-enterprise
25. Dwelly T, Maguire K, Truscott F and Thompson L (2006), *Under The Radar: Tracking and supporting rural home-based business*, LiveWork Network for the Commission for the Rural Communities. (Quoted in Carter *et al.*, 2009)
26. Newbery R and Bosworth G (2008), *Targeting the radar: exploring home based business. Paper presented to the annual conference of the Institute*

for Small Business and Entrepreneurship, Belfast 5–7 November. (Quoted in Carter et al, 2009)

Chapter 28

27. *COGS 2009 (Challenges and Opportunities for Growth and Sustainability).* A focus on women entrepreneurs by Delta Economics (supported by Women's Enterprise Centre of Excellence and Advantage West Midlands) www.deltaeconomics.com, p4, Go to COGS

Chapter 29

28. *COGS 2009 (Challenges and Opportunities for Growth and Sustainability).* A focus on women entrepreneurs by Delta Economics (supported by Women's Enterprise Centre of Excellence and Advantage West Midlands) www.deltaeconomics.com, p3, Go to COGS

FURTHER READING

Women entrepreneurs

How she does it: how women entrepreneurs are changing the rules of business success. Margaret Heffernan (Viking)

The Mumpreneur Guide: Start you own business. Antonia Chitty, Emma Cooper and Jess Williams (Ac Pr)

The Mumpreneur Diaries. Mosey Jones (Collins)

Supermummy: The ultimate mumpreneur's guide to online business success. Mel McGee (Lean Marketing Press)

Kitchen table tycoon: how to make it work as a mother and an entrepreneur. Anita Naik (Piatkus)

Women entrepreneurs: How ten leading businesswomen turned a good idea into a fortune. Sue Stockdale (Lean Marketing Press)

Inspiring women: 25 top female entrepreneurs. Michelle Rosenberg (Crimson Press)

Business as unusual: my entrepreneurial journey. Anita Roddick (Anita Roddick Books)

Make it your business. Bella Mehta and Lucy Martin (How To Books)

Making it: women entrepreneurs reveal their secrets of success. Lou Gimson and Alison Mitchell (Capstone)

Homeworking

Making it work at home. Anna Wright (Crimson Publishing)

Spare room startup. Emma Jones (Harriman House Publishing)

Freelance

Go freelance: how to succeed at being your own boss. (Steps to success). (A & C Black Publishers)

Go it alone: the streetwise secrets of self employment. Geoff Burch (Capstone)

How to make a million before lunch. Rachel Bridge (Virgin Books)

General

Business nightmares: hitting rock bottom and coming out on top. Rachel Elnaugh (Crimson Publishing)

Instant entrepreneur: the faster way to startup success. Robert Ashton (Prentice Hall Business)

Working for yourself (Which Guide). Mike Pywell and Bill Hilton (Which? Books)
Good small business guide 2010. (A&C Black)
The Small Business Start-Up Workbook. Cheryl D Rickman (How To Books)

Business planning
Guide to business planning. Graham Friend and Stefan Zehle (Economist Books)
How to write a business plan. Brian Finch (Kogan Page)

Coaching
Life Coaching, A Cognitive-Behavioural Approach. M Neenan and W Dryden (Routledge)

Marketing
A guide to promoting your business. Antonia Chitty, Emma Cooper and Jess Williams (Ac Pr.)
Powerful marketing on a shoestring budget: for small business. Dee Blick (Authorhouse)
Duct tape marketing: the world's most practical small business marketing guide. John Jantsch (Nelson Business)
Successful marketing for the small business: a practical guide. Dave Patten and (Institute of Directors/Kogan Page)
The ultimate guide to electronic marketing for small business. Tom Antion (John Wiley & Sons)
The new rules of marketing and PR. David Meerman Scott (John Wiley & Sons)

Accounts
Book-keeping and accounting for the small business: How to keep the books and maintain financial control over your business. Peter Taylor (How To Books)
Teach Yourself small business accounting. David Lloyd (Teach Yourself)
The Best Small Business Accounts Book: for a non-VAT registered business. Peter Hingston (Hingston Publishing)

Finance
Business finance theory and practice. Eddie McLaney (Financial Times/Prentice Hall)

Law
Business enterprise: law for the small business. Patricia Clayton (Kogan Page)

Franchising

How to evaluate a franchise. Martin Mendelsohn (Franchise World)
How to franchise your business. Martin Mendelsohn (British Franchise Association)
How to turn your business into the next global brand. Brian Duckett and Paul Monaghan (How To Books)
The 60-minute guide to franchising. Nigel Toplis and Geoff Marsh (The Sixty Minute Book Company Limited)
All available on www.thebfa.org/bookshop.asp

Direct selling

Direct selling: from door to door to network marketing. Richard Berry (out of print but available in public libraries) (Butterworth Heinemann)
Give it a go. Sonia Williams (available from www.showmummythemoney.com.au)

Social Enterprise

The Social Entrepreneur. Andrew Mawson (Atlantic Books)
The Power of Unreasonable People. John Elkington and Pamela Hartigan (Harvard Business School Press)

INDEX

Visit our How To website at **www.howto.co.uk**

At **www.howto.co.uk** you can engage in conversation with our authors – all of whom have 'been there and done that' in their specialist fields. You can get access to special offers and additional content but most importantly you will be able to engage with, and become a part of, a wide and growing community of people just like yourself.

At **www.howto.co.uk** you'll be able to talk and share tips with people who have similar interests and are facing similar challenges in their lives. People who, just like you, have the desire to change their lives for the better – be it through moving to a new country, starting a new business, growing their own vegetables, or writing a novel.

At **www.howto.co.uk** you'll find the support and encouragement you need to help make your aspirations a reality.

You can go direct to www.a-womans-guide-to-working-for-herself.co.uk which is part of the main How To site.

How To Books strives to present authentic, inspiring, practical information in their books. Now, when you buy a title from **How To Books,** you get even more than just words on a page.

the
information **store**

☎01603 773114
email: tis@ccn.ac.uk

21 DAY LOAN ITEM

Please return <u>on or before</u> the last date stamped above

CITY
COLLEGE
NORWICH

A fine will be charged for overdue items